Specters and Spirits
of the Appalachian
Foothills

Specters and Spirits of the Appalachian Foothills

James V. Burchill & Linda J. Crider

Rutledge Hill Press™
Nashville, Tennessee

A Division of Thomas Nelson, Inc.
www.ThomasNelson.com

Published by Rutledge Hill Press, a division of Thomas Nelson Inc., P.O. Box 141000, Nashville, Tennessee 37214.

Library of Congress Cataloging-in-Publication Data

Burchill, James V., 1930–
    Specters and spirits of the appalachian foothills / by James V. Burchill & Linda J. Crider.
        p. c.m.
    ISBN 1-55853-972-7
    1. Tales—Appalachian Region. 2. Legends—Appalachian Region. 3. Haunted places—Appalachian Region. I. Crider, Linda J., 1947– II. Title.
GR108 .B87 2002
398.2'0974—dc21   2002007369

Printed in the United States of America

02 03 04 05 06—5 4 3 2 1

This book is dedicated to the keepers of this good earth for their preservation of the southern Appalachian mountain ways of life, securing them for many generations yet to come.

Acknowledgements

Special thanks to the following for helping to make this book possible. Your stories have touched our hearts and our spirits:

Ann Arrington
Joanne Benson
Denise Bradburn
Clarice Beaver Chapman
Don, Fair & Cattrina Crider
Matthew, Karen,
  Terren & Jarreth
Melany Deeter
Alvin & Loraine Dunlap
Richard Dimsdale
Ernest Evans
Benny Hayes
Valerie Hudson
Chris Jones & Family
Janie Kincaid & Family
Martin Kroll
Alice Chapman Newgen

Sydney Prater
Ruth Roberts
Loretta Singleton
Dan & Wanda Stephenson
Marjorie & Billy Stephenson
Susan Thigpin
Claudia Townley & Family
Bess Watson
Mark Zanone
Mary Teems
Ruth Jones
Bob Burdick
James Buchanan
Crystal Newgen
Doug Swanson
Evelyn Prince Dockery
Joan Watkins

Many of the names of persons or places have been changed, as requested by the storyteller, for reasons of privacy.

Senses of Appalachia's Soul

I see you in my dreams
Just beyond my reach
I hear you in the night
Yet, don't know what you say
Your fragrance lingers lightly
I breathe deep to hold it close
I long for your touch
Your absent touch
Senses of Appalachia's soul
Need tending
Need mending
Need hope to stop the pain
A tearing of the soul
Isn't left without a scar
Mostly, it's just left
Hurting and alone
Then, it withers and dies
Creating a void in space and time
Echoing emptiness
Where once the reality of your presence
Made me complete

Introduction

Today's progress is tomorrow's heritage, but today's most prized heritage are our Appalachian legends. Our legends and stories, even those told in despair, inspire us, instilling a deeper love of family and the southern Appalachian mountain lands themselves.

Times here in Appalachia haven't always been easy and in many cases still aren't. But today the move is on to save as much of our heritage as we can. We begin with the stories and legends born here and passed down from one generation to another. In years to come, we hope they will be remembered. We also hope these stories stir your own memories and inspire you to tell your children your own family stories, keeping the legends alive and the art of oral history a part of family life.

These legends are as much a part of us as the blood of our ancestors that runs in our veins. Just as these legends are true to the mountains, so too do the spirits, just beyond sight and sound, cry out, lest they be forgotten—lost in time to forever float in the whisper of the southern Appalachian winds.

The collecting of haunting stories and legends by First Draft Writers Group began in 1990. Over the decade many old legends and newly experienced stories came our way. These stories and legends are priceless treasures, oral antiques in many cases. As one story piled atop another, memories were renewed and the storyteller was reminded of another time, perhaps another era when grandparents would entertain the children with stories their parents had told them concerning their own families. The telling strengthened the family bond, and many of these legends and stories have not lost their haunting flavor over the long years.

Children gasped as grandfather told how Herman heard screaming in the night, then mother would pass by the room and say, "Grandpa, don't scare the children so with those old family tales. They won't sleep a wink tonight." And often they did not sleep; instead, they insisted on hearing the story over and over as time passed.

The old legends and stories have influenced and helped make us the southern Appalachian people we are. They are a part of us. Our goal, perhaps our calling, is to be keepers of the spirited legends and stories in hopes they will be around for many generations yet to come. For these stories are here in these mountains, some as secret as hidden mountain gold; others drift about on the breezes in whispers. Some stories were told through tears and trembling voices, and a few brought the music of laughter. All the stories found within the pages of this book were told as truth by the storyteller.

These stories touch emotions and send questioning shivers up the spine. As in the first books, *Ghost and Haunts From the Appalachian Foothills* and *The Cold, Cold Hand*, this book was written in hopes of preserving part of the southern Appalachian heritage born here in mountains as old as time.

I remember once, a long, long time ago, when Grandpa told me about a place way up on Stover's mountain . . .

The Red-Haired Woman

The old River Road that runs alongside of the Ocoee River between Cleveland, Tennessee, and Murphy, North Carolina, has always been treacherous. Its narrow twisting curves crawl through the gorge like a black snake. The high rock wall on one side of the gorge is scarred, scraped, and rubbed smooth in places as trucks and cars, over the years, rode the wall and the asphalt pavement through the sharp, hair-pin curves.

The River Road has been the place of automobile accidents since its early beginnings. It has birthed stories and legends of mangled bodies, as well as minds. And once it was the sight of countless little wooden crosses that marked death sites of travelers whose lives never left that winding narrow road that snaked through the gorge.

One story has been told over the last half-century about a red-haired woman whose body was never found though her car was discovered in the river next to the old power station. It was smashed and crushed, giving credence to the old saying, "Nobody could have got out of there alive." Authorities at the accident site believed the car was traveling at a high rate of speed. It first hit the wall then was knocked across the road to plunge down into the icy mountain Ocoee River waters.

Even though the red-haired woman's body was never

recovered, she has been seen by many as they traveled this stretch of road. It's said she appears in the back seats of automobiles and warns drivers of the dangers ahead. Her reflection in the rear-view mirror is seen as a translucent spirit. She has never evoked fear in those who have seen her. One man has told of his experience with the red-haired woman many times over the years, and it has become well known in the area.

John Kline was a young man born and raised on the North Carolina-Tennessee-Georgia border in a small rural community known as Murphy, North Carolina. While stationed at an Air Force base in Arkansas, John was called home because his mother was dying. As he made arrangements to take immediate leave, he received another urgent call from his sister, who, through her sobs, told the young man that their mother was asking for him. Though the family remained hopeful, they feared that the old woman would not last until John could get home.

It was nearing one o'clock in the afternoon when John left the military base. Anxious, he pushed the speed limit in his old car as he made his way toward the Arkansas-Tennessee state line. He didn't stop along the way for anything but to fill the car's gas tank. He called home from a pay phone as an attendant filled the car with gas, checked the oil, and cleaned the windshield. His mother was still alive, but just barely. The doctors had arrived, but they were helpless to do anything. Friends, neighbors, and family were there taking turns standing vigil around the sick bed, assuring the old woman she wasn't alone and that her son was on his way.

John had been on the road for fourteen hours and was near exhaustion, but he knew he would be home in little more than an hour when he left Cleveland, Tennessee, taking the old River Road. The mountain air was chilly, and John rolled up the car's window when a light rain began to fall. Even though he was bone weary from the drive, he was afraid he'd never get to see his mother alive, so he pushed the accelerator to the floor. He knew it was foolish to drive so fast, but time was now his enemy. Rounding a hairpin curve near the power dam, John caught a glimpse of a red-haired woman in the back seat of his car from the rear view mirror.

"Slow down," she said. "There's no need to hurry. Your mother is dead."

Then as suddenly as the woman had appeared, she was gone. As the words echoed in John's mind, he glanced at the dashboard clock. It read 3:30 a.m. Slowing his speed, John realized, was the sensible thing to do lest he not get home at all. Within the hour he pulled into the driveway of his old home place. His sister met him at the door.

"She's gone, John," she cried, wrapping her arms around the brother stepping into the house. "She just couldn't hang on any longer." John held his sister close, and he too cried as they shared the loss of their mother. Later, John asked his sister when their mother had died. She answered, "It was 3:30; I know because the clock struck then, marking the half hour."

It was the exact same time the red-haired woman had appeared in the car with John and told him not to hurry because his mother was dead.

The Poker Game

Legend has it, says Richard Dimsdale, that the weekly poker game was held at Earl Johnson's Pig Parlor. Every Saturday night from 1916 to 1921, Earl's friends—lawyer Jacob Washburn and wealthy merchants Roger Wells, Christian Wolfert, and Herbert Horan—played by lantern light as there was no rural electricity in the north Georgia mountains at that time. Earl was said to be a rich man who didn't trust banks and had his stash hidden somewhere in his house. One cool autumn night, the five friends were playing cards and drinking 'shine when some men, no one knows how many, burst into Johnson's large farmhouse.

The next day, Sunday, Mrs. Wells went to the sheriff's office. She was crying that her husband, Roger, never returned from his weekly poker session. Sheriff Edgar Bankhead and Deputy Hoss Martin went to the pig parlor and found carnage. All the poker players were dead, beheaded. There were no clues, and no trace of the murderers was ever found. The case was never solved.

"I heard the story of the poker game slaughter early on," says the now middle-aged Richard. "My grandpa told me of the murders, and as a boy I was scared to go by the pig parlor. It was at the end of a dirt road about three miles from our place." Earl Johnson had no living relatives, at least none were ever found. So the farm and house had fallen into disrepair. "What my folks didn't tell me was the legend that went with the old Johnson place. When I was not more than a boy, I found it out for myself.

"My cousin, Mark, and a friend of his, Jacky Stamey, wanted to go to the scene of the murders and beheadings that had happened so many years ago. We drove down the dirt road. It was a Saturday night, not quite dark yet, as we stopped in front of Earl Johnson's farmhouse. It was a large, two-story house, and where we were standing we could look through the windows into the front room. 'You're not going to believe what's going to happen tonight,' said Jacky, 'at least that's what my older brother told me.'

"It was about 9:30 p.m. when Mark said, 'Look.' I did, and what I saw were four lights in the living room, and then a fifth light. It glowed from the porch not twenty feet away in an eerie haze. Now at first I thought the guys were pulling a trick on me, but they looked as scared as I was. We stayed for a while then left. When I arrived home, I asked my dad about the lights. 'Yes, son,' he said, 'you did see lights. I've seen them many times. The legend is that the four lights in the living room are ghosts of four of the poker players. The fifth light, the one on the porch and swinging a lantern, is one of the five standing guard for the other players.'

"Well," said Richard, "over the years, I, too, saw the lights many times. But only on Saturday night."

Face on the Door

In past years, small hospitals sprang up in many rural counties across the southern Appalachian foothills. Some had as many as ten two-bed rooms and a four-bed ward. Whenever possible, one private room, a suite, was made available to serve the needs of those patients needing isolation. The medical facilities served the small communities well for many years. Then as time passed and specialized medicines began to appear at the larger city hospitals and transportation became more readily available, folks just stopped going to the small county hospitals. Some of the facilities were turned into nursing homes for the elderly with no family to tend their needs. Others became middle schools, and still more became office buildings. But in their time, these rural hospitals were highly acclaimed and indeed served the medical needs of their communities.

Strange stories have always been connected to hospitals in the southern Appalachian foothills. Perhaps this comes from all the births, deaths, and frightful sufferings of illness between the two. One hospital in east Tennessee was said to have been haunted for years by a long dead patient who was moved to a better room, much against his will. Mr. Potter was old, well into his eighties, and suffering from cancer. His severe pain at times caused him to scream out.

But since he was terminal, there was little the doctors could do for him except try to keep his pain at a minimal level by injecting him with strong painkillers.

His three sons were married with children of their own. On Sundays they never missed a visit with the dying man. The hospital staff knew this shuffling in and out of family members upset their patient, but couldn't deny them visitation. After all, it helped the family feel better knowing they had not deserted their eldest member. It was discussed and decided, after several Sunday visits, that Mr. Potter would be moved into the suite. There, he wouldn't disturb a roommate (even though his present roommate, Mr. King, was senile and deaf and hardly realized anything was going on around him). The hospital staff felt that both patients would be better off. The suite could accommodate Mr. Potter's family on their Sunday visits, instead of their having to gather in the hall as they had been, talking or sitting in straight-back chairs lining the wall. It was also decided that being in a larger, private room might lessen some of Mr. Potter's agitation, for in his discomfort he was beginning to speak harshly to his nurses. With the decision made, Mr. Potter was told about his move into the new suite at the end of the hall that would take place the very next day.

But Mr. Potter screamed and screamed. He did not want to leave the security of what had become familiar to him. The staff saw this outburst as anxiety and figured once the old man was settled in the room, he would enjoy being there and it would afford his family easier Sunday visits. The room even had a television, which would allow him a pleasant way to pass the time when the pain wasn't so bad. All afternoon the old man continued to scream. He screamed from the pain, but mostly, he screamed from anger. Shouting for the nurses, he begged to stay where he was. Then he threatened. "I'll die if you move me out of this room," he'd yell. "You wait and see. I'll die. I promise you. And you'll all be sorry, cause I won't forget."

The nurses continued to care for their patient, paying little attention to his ravings, and the next day they did indeed move the old man to the suite. Once there, with its wallpapered walls and double windows that let in much more sunlight, the old man became quiet. He rarely made a sound at all. Only his eyes showed signs of life, and they were filled with hatred as he glared icily at the nurses that came and went from his room. The next morning, after the shift change, as Mr. Potter was having his blood pressure checked, he looked up at the nurse and through a weak smile said, "You'll be sorry." Later, when breakfast was brought to the suite, the old man was found dead. He had indeed kept his promise.

A few weeks later, housekeeping reported to one of the nurses that a face had appeared on the door of Mr. Potter's first room. It was the spitting image of the old man himself. Hurrying to see, the nursing staff agreed it was indeed Mr. Potter's true likeness there in the grain of the wood. Remembering the old man's words, the nurses became anxious and the door was changed, but the likeness soon appeared on the new door. Three times the door was changed, and every time Mr. Potter's image glared out from the grain of the wood. Sometimes strange sounds could be heard coming from the room even though it was empty. Even later, after the room was converted to a storage closet, the noises continued. Occasionally the call light above the door would come on, blinking to notify nurses of assistance needed in the room. Mr. Potter had kept his promise, and the staff was reminded of it every day with his image on the door, his ghostly moaning, and his summoning of the nurses with the blinking call light.

Office space now occupies the hospital facility. It's been said by some of the workers there that that particular room has an uneasy feel to it and that occasionally foot-steps can be heard when there is no one there at all.

The Crying Statue

Haunted cemetery stories have been around these old mountains as long as the dead. They're told over and over, and youths often test the stories by visiting the resting places of the dead in the dark of night. Some have found evidence that gives credence to some of those old stories. But there are others who never speak of apparitions seen, voices heard, or experiences witnessed.

One such story comes from a very old cemetery in Cobb County. Some of the gravestones are giant statues with intricate engraved words about the deceased buried beneath them; others are mere rocks with no words—no record of the life, not even the name, of the soul who lies beneath the dark cold earth. Yet one gravestone is noted for its haunting sadness. It is said that in the late 1800s, a child died and was buried there. The mother, devastated beyond all measure, almost lost her mind. To ease her pain, a gravestone was commissioned that showed her holding the child lovingly in her arms. Weather-worn and mottled gray with lichen and mold, the stone still marks the small grave. It has been told for years and witnessed by many that at certain times, when the moon is full and lights the dark of night, that stone woman cries tears down on the stone child she holds close to her heart.

Some have heard faint crying, but whether from the child or the mother they do not know. The tears, though, are the mother's, and they glisten in their wetness as they course down her stone cheeks. In her undying sorrow, the sad mother has mourned the loss of her beloved child for almost a hundred years, and if the stone stands for a hundred more, she will continue to weep when the moon is full and lights the night sky.

The Cutter Legend

The Cutter Legend started on a cool moonlit night in October 1905. Nothing much is known about what happened that night since only two people witnessed it, and they refuse to talk about it. Hoyt Cutter, the father, was a moonshiner, not by choice but by necessity. He had to feed his family, and moonshining was the only way he knew how to do it. A religious man, Hoyt never drank the stuff himself. He and his wife Amy had three children, Sarah, Rainey, and Josh. Hoyt was forty-three.

A few years earlier, at seventeen, Sarah had married a local boy, Grady Watson. Wanting to keep the family close, Hoyt and Amy built Sarah and Grady a cabin at the foot of the mountain, not more than a quarter-mile from Sarah's place of birth. In 1904, Sarah bore a son, Paul. But early in 1905, Grady began to drink moonshine quite heavily. Then he started to batter Sarah. After one of Grady's drunken bouts, Sarah and the baby moved back up the mountain with her parents. She loved Grady, but when he was drunk, he was mean and vile.

The night the legend began, Hoyt was "going down to Sarah's place to pray over Grady." Sarah's brother Rainey went along, too. The two men walked down the trail toward Sarah and Grady's home.

11

"Pa, I hear someone shouting," said Rainey.

"Yes," answered his father, "I hear it too." It sounded like Grady was screaming, and they could hear another voice, guttural and roaring. They ran around the bend and stopped dead in their tracks. Fifteen minutes later they were back in their own house. Both men, ashen-faced, refused to say anything about what they had seen or what had happened. When Hoyt and Rainey awoke the next morning, the hair on their heads had turned snow white. Hoyt, Rainey, and Sarah went into town to the sheriff's office. And that was all anyone knew about the Cutter Legend, although rumors ran rampant through the small settlements in the north Georgia mountains.

On a warm sunny day in October 1998, the leaves in the mountains sported their autumn colors and an old man sat on his porch. His eyes were bright and knowing as he lit a cigarette. "Yes, I know," he said with a strong voice. "I know a body shouldn't smoke. But heck, I'm ninety-four years old." He wore overalls, and an Atlanta Braves baseball cap covered his graying hair. He smiled sadly, "I'm going to tell all about the Cutter Legend. I am the only one who knows what happened that night so many years ago." With a twinkle in his eyes, he lit another cigarette and said, "For you see, my name is Paul Cutter, not Watson. My mother, Sarah, had my name and hers legally changed to Cutter. Back in 1956, when I was fifty-two years old, I went to my Uncle Rainey's home and demanded he tell me what happened to my father, Grady Watson. Here is what he told me:

When we, Pa and me, got down to the flat, we heard loud voices. One was Grady's, and he was screaming curses at someone, or something. The other voice had an evil, horrible sound to it. We couldn't understand what the other voice was roaring. We turned around the bend, and there was Grady; he was, well, he was jumping around like he was dancing a jig. In the moonlight we could see his face,

12

and he looked vicious. He was jumping around and cursing. Then we saw it, a figure on Grady's back, faceless.

"Kneel, Boy!" Pa said, "and pray like you never prayed before."

"What is it, Pa?" I asked.

"It's the Devil. Grady's got the Devil on his back," Pa answered.

We knelt and prayed. But the voices continued cursing one another. I looked up once and saw Grady spinning around as if to throw his enemy off his back, but he couldn't. Then there was silence. I felt Pa nudge me, and we stood. Grady was gone; there was no sign of him anywhere. So we went home, and the next day we went to the sheriff's office.

The sheriff heard our story, and the four of us went back to the trail. On the way, we stopped at Grady and Sarah's cabin. Inside, it was completely destroyed; nothing was left unbroken. Later a sheriff's deputy brought two bloodhounds and gave them Grady's scent from his clothes. The hounds tore up the trail and stopped at the spot we last saw Grady, and they whined. They would not go any farther, and no one ever saw Grady Watson again.

Paul Cutter finished his tale by telling how the next day his grandfather burned down the cabin where Paul had been born. The old man lit another cigarette, sighed, and said, "I don't know what it was that got my father. There was no blood found or any other trace of what happened to him. But there is one more thing. I doubt if it has anything to do with it, but the date of my father's disappearance was October 31, 1905, Halloween night. In those days, folks in the mountains believed demons of hell ran amok, taking souls back to the bowels of hell on Halloween Night."

Lantern Hill

The old Civil War battlefields are bathed in glory and written up in history books for their victories and defeats. Yet much of what occurred on those bloody fields is known only through the stories handed down from generation to generation. And a few things, apparitions caught in the reflections of time, are spoken of only when they are witnessed today.

The Daniel brothers, Billy and Stephen, and two cousins, Jim and Carl, were out one Saturday night near the Chickamauga Battlefield State Park. Although it was dark as soot, they decided to stop and drink a six-pack of beer. It was a warm, muggy, summer night, and thunder rumbled loud in the distance like some long-ago cannon fire. It was evident one of those nasty summer storms, so common in the Appalachian foothills, would soon send the boys home. They parked and got out of the car. Carl sprawled on the hood of the old Ford, Jim and Billy squatted on the ground, and Stephen leaned against a big Oak tree. They all had a beer and planned the next week's fishing trip up the Little Tennessee. A flip of a coin determined that Carl and Billy took the last two beers. Stephen was reminding the others about fish bait when he leaned to one side as if to get a better view of something fronting him there in the darkness.

"Hey, Guys," he whispered. "Check this out. What is that?" The others turned to look in the direction Stephen was facing. Coming down the side of a hill was a light. It glowed and seemed to rock sideways as it raced down the hill. Before it reached the bottom, lightning cracked the sky, thunder shook the valley, and the light was gone.

"What was that?" Billy asked.

"Don't know," said Carl, "but it's gonna storm. We better go."

The boys scrambled into the car. All looked back at the hill, trying to see what had made the eerie light. There was nothing, not even when Stephen turned the car so the headlights shone in the right direction. A shiver gripped Jim, "This is spooky. Let's get out of here." And with that, the boys sped out of the park.

Stephen later heard that the hill was called Lantern Hill, and during the Civil War, a soldier was appointed to stand guard at the top of the hill. If he saw anything suspicious, he was to run down the hill and warn the troops below. One night the soldier standing guard went to sleep and woke suddenly to discover the enemy approaching the camp of sleeping soldiers. Grabbing his lantern, he began to run down the hill, swinging it from side to side as warning, hoping someone would see it and wake the sleeping regiment. But before the young soldier could reach the bottom of the hill, a sniper's bullet killed him. His warning never reached the camp.

The light has been seen by many over the years. It is believed the young Civil War soldier is still trying to warn the camp of the enemy's approach lest they all be killed because he fell asleep at his post.

The Witch
in the Hollow

Lily Young was in love. She thought Grady Holmes was the answer to her prayers. It was 1946, and the Youngs lived in the northern section of Fanin County, Georgia. They were a close-knit family and every Sunday could be found in church. Now, no one in Lily's family thought the moonshiner Grady was right for her. Hilda, Lily's mother, was especially firm in her commitment that the ne'er-do-well Grady would not marry her lovely daughter. But every evening Lily would go down by the creek and meet her Prince Charming. Lily said all along that no matter what, she was going to marry Grady Holmes.

Finally, Hilda said drastic measures must be taken, so she called her Aunt Marge who lived over in Gilmer County. Most folks in the Appalachian foothills know of an Aunt Marge. Most had one like her in the family or knew of the type—a take-charge, no-nonsense woman who was the boss of her family. When Aunt Marge arrived and heard the tale of Lily's love for the moonshiner, she decided immediately what must be done.

"We will go see Miss Parry," said Aunt Marge, "that is, if she's still alive."

"But she's a witch," moaned Hilda, "at least that's what folks around here say."

"So," snarled Aunt Marge, "maybe that's what we need in this situation."

Miss Parry (no one knew her first name) lived up an old dirt road way up in a hollow. Nobody knew much about her; she was so old she had outlived her contemporaries and had no family left. Although there was no proof she was a witch, as many locals claimed, people who lived in the mountains went to her when they had troubles. And according to these local folks, she always came through. So one bright sunny afternoon, Hilda and Aunt Marge drove up the pitiful dirt road to Miss Parry's shack.

"We arrived at the shack," says Hilda Young, "and it was a shack. It looked like a good wind would blow it into the next county. We went up a rickety porch and knocked. The door opened, and Miss Parry invited us to come in. Miss Parry was small and bony; her nose was hooked, and her gray hair was sparse, barely covering her scalp. Her skin was dark brown like parchment, and she looked older than anybody I ever saw, but her eyes were bright and glowed with delight.

"After we told her our problem, she said, 'So Lily wants to marry Grady Holmes?'

"'We don't want Lily to marry that no-account,' said Aunt Marge.

"Miss Parry stared for a bit then she mixed some dry stuff together. It looked like twigs. She chanted something we couldn't understand over the pot holding the now foul-smelling brew. The old woman cackled, 'Don't fret about it none. Lily won't marry Grady Holmes.'

"We left after that statement and went home. That evening Lily went down to the creek where she usually met Grady. He didn't show up, but Lily wasn't concerned; sometimes her beloved couldn't make it. The next day Aunt Marge and I went shopping. We went into the General Store and it was packed, and everyone seemed to be talking at once. I asked Mr. Howell, the clerk, 'What's all the commotion about?'

"'Well,' answered the clerk, 'Grady Holmes got killed yesterday afternoon. Seems Holmes was trucking some moonshine across to Chatsworth when the law took off after him. He must have been going ninety miles an hour when he lost control. He slammed into a tree and the car exploded. He was burned to a crisp.'

"'What time did this happen?' asked Aunt Marge.

"'Oh, according to the sheriff, it was exactly 3:10 yesterday afternoon.'

"As we left the store, Aunt Marge said, 'You know, Hilda, we got to Miss Parry's house about three yesterday afternoon. I guess Miss Parry is a witch.'"

Lily, after the shock of Grady's death, gradually returned to normal. Three years later, she married Johnny Potter. She and Johnny had been in school together, and when he returned from military service, he'd begun courting Lily. Lily is now a great-grandmother.

The Restaurant

Susan Cantrell, a young college student working as a waitress in the 1840 Restaurant, adjusts her mop cap, pats her historical costume, and tells the story of a young girl who waited in that same structure for the return of her soldier and lover.

"The 1840 Restaurant was a mansion built in 1840 by the Allen family. The Allens lived in the three-story rough-hewn log home until the last of the family died. It had many rooms and on the outside looks much as it did the day it was built. The Allens had three children. Tom, the oldest, died at the Battle of Bull Run. Chandra, the second child, died in 1858 of pneumonia, at the age of twenty-two. Catherine, the youngest, was engaged in 1861 to a young man named Jerome Hartsfield. They were, so the story is told, very much in love. When the Civil War broke out, Jerome was offered a commission in the Confederate Army. With many tears, Catherine saw her beloved off to war.

"In 1863, Jerome came home, a shell of his former self. Catherine didn't care; she took him in. Both her parents had passed away, and except for the servants, she lived alone. When it was time for Jerome to go back to war, his health had improved quite a bit. He was ready to fight again. However, Catherine beseeched him to stay; he could, she said, hide out

19

at the log home. The house and farm were situated in the southwestern section of Virginia in a sparsely populated area where no one would ever find him. But Jerome, duty-conscious, went back to his regiment. He arrived just in time for several major battles and was killed in action by a sniper's bullet.

"Catherine did not believe her lover was dead. Every night at 10 o'clock, after she'd retired for the night, the servants could hear her wailing, 'Oh, Jerome, come back to me. Please come back.'"

Inside the restaurant are many rooms. Some are gift shops; some are historical exhibits with paintings of the Allen family. There is even one of Captain Jerome Hartsfield. There are eight private dining rooms. Strangely, the management accepts no reservations past 8:30 p.m. All diners and employees must be out of the building by 9:30. The management insists on this. If perchance anyone is still in the building at 10 p.m., they're likely to hear a wailing, then some sobs, and a voice crying out, "Jerome, please come back!" Many guests and employees have heard these ghostly sounds, but the manager says, "Let poor Catherine Allen have her time to mourn her lost lover, Jerome."

Hell's Storms

Storms in the mountain foothills of north Georgia are common occurrences in the spring and fall as one season gives over to the next. But the storms in the spring of 1994 will be forever remembered for the devastation left in their wake. No words can describe the horror of tornadic storms gone mad. Hell's demons themselves are said to be let loose on all creation. For whatever reason, certain areas of North Georgia are targets for nature's wrath.

Ben Hayes, a physical therapist assistant working with home-bound patients, heard many stories of horror and destruction after nature's siege through Cherokee and Pickens counties on one infamous Palm Sunday.

"Everything was near destroyed in the little settlement of Jerusalem. Homes, barns, chicken houses, stores; nothing was left but splinters," said Ben. "And the destruction wasn't isolated to just that one area. The storm appeared to be everywhere at once, all over the county, taking what it wanted, and it must have wanted all that the people had. Yet some were lucky, some were spared." Ben sighed and shook his head wearily. His eyes sad, he went on with his story.

"Occasionally, you would see a single house untouched, and for a quarter of a mile around it, not even a tree would be left standing. In one house, the pictures hanging on the walls weren't even out of place, but the house across the road didn't have a foundation left. It was painfully sad, unreal, like something you see on television that happens somewhere else to nobody you know."

*   *   *

The survivors tell their stories in voices filled with pain and loss. Some heard it coming, a few saw its approach, but the strangest words came from a little girl, Heather, who was about seven years old. As the day grew hotter and the humidity grew heavy, Heather stood in the back doorway, trying to catch a breeze. The skies were quickly turning angry and the air heavy. Dora, the mother, was watching television, trying to get a weather report, as it was obvious something bad was about to happen. The weather channel reported that conditions were rapidly changing and the tornado watch had been upgraded to a warning. The spokesman on the television screen advised all persons in Pickens and Cherokee counties to seek shelter, for a tornado had indeed been spotted and reported. It was heading northeast. Dora called to Heather, but the little girl did not respond. Dora hurried to the kitchen to find the child staring across the mountain foothills to the west.

"Hurry, Heather. We have to get in the hallway. Close the door," the woman commanded nervously. The child remained transfixed. "Heather," Dora shouted, grabbing the child by the shoulders and jerking her around. "Now. Heather, go to the hall. A tornado is coming." The little girl blinked her eyes several times at the woman before her as if she hadn't heard a word her mother had said. Dora grabbed the child up in her arms and ran to the darkened hallway just as the electricity cracked loudly and went off. Heather was cold and trembling; Dora thought it was from fear. She tried to soothe her baby. "Don't be afraid," she said, rubbing the child's long curly hair and holding her close. Thunder rumbled louder.

"I saw the devil, Mama," said Heather in a near whisper. "I really did."

"What?" Dora asked, puzzled.

"I saw the devil. He was dressed all in black with a hood on his long coat covering his head. He was above the big mountain looking at me," the little girl said. "Then he looked at everything else and raised his arms up."

"No. No, Heather," said Dora, "you didn't see the devil. That was just the wind blowing big trees or maybe even a funnel cloud." Dora pulled her child even closer and held her tightly.

"Yes, Mama, I really did," Heather cried. Instantly, the roar of a thousand trains sounded, and Dora covered Heather with her own body there in the hallway of their small home as the darkness surrounding them turned a smoky green and smelled of sulphur for what seemed an eternity but was surely only seconds. Then the smoke and the odor just faded away.

It was over, and they had lived. The roof was partially gone as was most everything else. But the memory of seeing the devil over the high mountain before the storm hit will remain with Heather, perhaps, forever.

*   *   *

Another horrible storm took place in the Yellow Creek area back in 1974. Lots of homes were destroyed, and several people were killed. But this storm, too, left strange stories behind, stories almost too strange to be true.

When the violent tornado had passed, help came. Most everything was destroyed and gone. Many people were hurt, some killed, and it took time to get the people taken care of, but when they had been seen to, it was discovered the little community church had also been destroyed; the walls and windows, roof, floor, and doors were gone. Yet the pulpit still stood where it always had, and the big church Bible lay atop it, untouched—not even wet from the torrential rains. It was still opened to the scriptures used in the preacher's last sermon.

The Visitor

Dan Stephenson shared more than one story on the day of storytelling. This one concerned his daughter Sherry, her husband, David, and her three-year-old child, Halley.

They were living in a mobile home in Georgia near the Tennessee border not far from Chattanooga. One night while lying in bed they heard footsteps walking through their living room. David jumped out of bed and rushed out to the living room. He didn't see anything and returned to bed. Two nights later they again heard footsteps, but no one was there or anywhere else on the property when David checked. This went on for several weeks until one night the footsteps were heavier and louder. Sherry awakened her husband, and together they checked each room—nothing. Still, they could hear the heavy footsteps heading toward Halley's room. They rushed in to find only Halley there, sound asleep in her bed. The little girl woke and yawned, and when her parents asked if she'd seen anyone, she replied, "I didn't see anybody but William." Much as they tried, they couldn't get anything else out of little Halley. She yawned again and turned her back to her parents and went to sleep.

One week later, on a bright autumn afternoon, Sherry was doing the dishes when she heard the footsteps again.

The sound went down the hallway through the living room and stopped at the entranceway. Halley was out in the yard playing, and Sherry tore out of the trailer to get her. Halley was standing in her playpen looking up and talking.

"Halley," asked Sherry, "who are you talking to?"

"William," answered Halley.

"But Halley, there is no one here," said Sherry.

"Yes there is. It's William. He's right here," insisted Halley. Sherry tried time and again to convince Halley they were alone, but Halley continued to look up and talk to the invisible apparition named William that only Halley could see.

Sherry and her father, Dan Stephenson, are convinced the invisible William was Dan's father and Sherry's grandfather, who said he'd come back if possible. His name was William, and he never saw his great-granddaughter—while he was alive, anyway.

The Baby
and the Blonde

Dan Stephenson doesn't believe in ghosts, haunts, spirits, or any other spooky thing. Dan believes all those ghostly things folks see are really energy, energy people left behind when they passed over from this life to the next. Dan, however, had a strange thing happen, actually two things, and they just might be related. When Dan married, he and his bride, Wanda, moved into a small apartment. They had not been living there long when Dan, sitting at the kitchen table, spotted a small girl standing between him and the kitchen stove.

"Who are you?" asked Dan, not quite sure what to do. The little girl, who Dan guessed was about eight years old, paid no attention to him. Dan asked again, "Can I help you?" Still, there was no response from the little girl. And then she vanished. Dan walked over to where she had stood, and it was the strangest thing, the spot where she stood was cold, so cold that Dan started shivering. This happened two more times, but Wanda never saw the little girl. About a week later, something else happened that couldn't be explained.

"We had just gone to bed," says Dan, "when I heard footsteps walking across the parlor floor.

27

"'Dan,' cried Wanda, 'there is someone in the front room.'

"We went out of the bedroom," continued Dan, "and what we saw was a stunning young blonde woman dressed in a silky nightgown. She walked down the hall toward the kitchen and disappeared.

"'Who is that?' Wanda laughed to cover her chilly fear, 'One of your old girlfriends?'"

Dan had no idea who the woman was, but later that night they heard the sound of a young girl crying. "Mama, Mama, where are you?" the voice echoed through the apartment. The next night Dan went into the kitchen, and there was the little girl again. She paid no heed to Dan, but this time she cried out, "Mama, Mama." When the girl faded away, he ran to where she'd stood, and once again the space was ice cold. Shivers ran up his back as he went down the hallway, only to see the blonde woman, still dressed in the silky nightgown, coming toward him.

"Hey," he yelled, but she vanished instantly. Dan couldn't figure out what was going on, so every evening he would sit long hours, sometimes until daylight, trying to catch either the little girl or the blonde woman. He was on his umpteenth cup of coffee one night when he heard "Mama, Mama," and it sounded much louder now. The child seemed to be crying out in desperation. Before he could do anything, the strange blonde woman walked into the kitchen and headed straight to the girl. "Mama, please, Mama!" the child shouted. Dan sat stunned as the woman gently put her arms around the girl and both were instantly gone. When he went to the place where they had stood, the cold spot was gone. Dan never saw the woman or the child again.

"I don't know what I saw," said Dan. "But I still don't believe in . . . well, ghosts."

Pine Top School

It was not uncommon in times past for the settlement church house to serve also as the school. As rural transportation to and from the schools had not yet come into being and roads were little more than rutted wagon trails, the students walked. Sometimes they walked several miles a day to the one-room church-school, and students of all ages and grade levels shared space and a teacher. The teacher generally boarded with one of the students' families and was most times paid a small wage. Big pot-bellied stoves centered the high-ceiling rooms and were fueled with wood cut by the older boys. When the heat became oppressive in the late days of May, classes were often taken out of doors. Older children were expected to tutor younger ones and help look after them. Most children were eager to learn, and schooling was taken very seriously by students, as well as by their parents.

As time passed, many schools were built near those churches. The children still played among the gravestones, drank water from the same springs, and used the same outdoor toilets. One such later-built school was called Pine Top, same as the church some hundred yards away. Considered quite up-to-date in the early 1950s, the school had eight classrooms and a teacher for each, indoor plumbing, including two restrooms and a large cafeteria where lunches were served for ten cents. Soon after the new school was opened and classes began, cold spots were noticed, spots that even the new steam radiators couldn't warm in the winter. These cold spots would send shivers down the spine even on the hottest days of summer. Teachers and students alike felt these chills, yet nobody could explain them.

Belda Osgood, one of the lunchroom workers, always came to work with her husband, Gentry, Pine Top's janitor. In winter, Gentry kept the furnaces stoked and tried to keep up with the general cold-weather maintenance. In warmer weather, he repaired playground equipment and unstopped the seemingly forever backed-up plumbing, caused by spring rains overfilling the septic system.

One warm May morning the couple came in early, even before the sun was up bright. Gentry was faced with a leak in the second-grade classroom. The ceiling was brown with ugly water stains. For some reason, the ceiling dripped water long after all the rains had stopped. Belda brewed coffee in a small enamel coffee pot brought from home. When it was ready, she poured two cups; hearing a noise in the storeroom, she called to her husband. No answer. But she could see light streaming from the opened doorway.

"Gentry," she called again, "coffee's ready." Still there was no answer. Fearing something was wrong, Belda hurried to the storeroom just down a short hallway. When she stepped into the room, she saw a child, a little girl in a long blue dress with white collar and cuffs. Her shoes were brown brogans over white socks. She had long yellow curls and wide blue eyes; a slight smile graced her lips. Her skin was white as cream, and she held her arms out and her palms up. Balls of light bounded from her palms up and out to dance about the room. Shocked at the sight before her, Belda called to the child. But the girl never moved, just stared at her hands, as more balls of light appeared to jump from her palms. Belda called again, "Little girl," and stepped closer to the child. The child never looked at the woman, yet when Belda took another step toward her, the child faded away and the dancing balls of light soon followed. Gentry found Belda leaning against the door facing, scared and trembling.

Later that same day a little boy in the second grade refused to participate in "circle time," saying a little girl with long yellow curls and wearing a long blue dress with white at the neck and ends of her sleeves was sitting in his place. He became very upset that no one but him could see her.

The cold spots got colder after that, and some special people were called in to investigate. It was reported that they could indeed feel, yet not explain, the ten- to twenty-degree temperature difference in certain parts of the school, nor could they explain the brown spots found on all the walls, ceiling, and floor of the storage room. The little girl was seen occasionally by those at the school, usually in the storage room or in the second-grade classroom. Sometimes, students would turn quickly to see who was laughing, only to find no one there. Once the school even closed for a few years. Some believe it was because of the mysterious ghost child although the official reason was that attendance was too low to keep the school open. But after a few years, it did reopen and the reports of a ghost child at the school continued to circulate. No one ever knew who the ghost child might be or why she lingered at Pine Top.

Time passed, schools consolidated, and Pine Top is now gone, but Belda says no one could have come inside the school building that morning as Gentry had locked the door behind them. She wonders about the child with the long yellow curls surrounded by dancing lights and what the people called in to investigate really discovered. For that was not the only time they were called to investigate apparitions and cold spots at Pine Top.

The Crater Mansion

Over the years, the Crater Mansion has seen many strange things. Completed in 1912, it sits in Cullman County, in northern Alabama near Tennessee. Two sisters, Irene and Jane, and their brother, Willard, lived in the large family home until their deaths. Jane went first in 1937, then Irene in 1940. Willard died in 1943. None of the Craters had married, so with no heirs, the mansion soon deteriorated. Built of granite imported from Maine, the outside did not change, but the inside became a mess.

Then in 1979, a consortium bought the old place and restoration was started. Finally, the old Crater Mansion was restored to its former glory. Inside, the three-story home sparkled with new paint. All the rooms were filled with genuine antiques, and the dining room stood waiting as if the Craters would be coming to dinner soon. The dual staircases were all restored, and the verandas looked as though Vern and Irene, or maybe Fred and Ginger, would dance across them any minute. As added attraction, six cabins were built on the spacious grounds. These, modern as tomorrow, the consortium planned to rent by the day to guests who wanted a quiet weekend. And the guests could browse through the mansion to their hearts' content.

"However," said Genelle Bane, "all did not go according

to plan. My husband, Tony, and I decided to spend a weekend at the Crater Mansion before we moved into our new house. We arrived on a Friday evening. It was June 1987. The cabin was perfect. It had everything, including a spa. We were thrilled. It looked like it was going to be a perfect weekend. Tony had gone outside to bring in our luggage, and as I entered the bedroom, I felt a hand brush my hair. I thought it was Tony, and I smiled as I turned, but Tony wasn't there. No one was. I didn't say anything to Tony; I thought maybe it was just my imagination.

"We came back to the cabin after dinner. We were met by Mr. Patterson, the manager of the mansion property. He invited us to tour the large Crater Mansion. Delighted by his invitation, we took him up on his offer to be our guide. We strolled through the sitting rooms and the large dining room where the colors were bright with an abundance of red. Two staircases led up to a large balcony, and a hallway led to the six bedrooms, three on each side. Tony and Mr. Patterson walked to the left, while I casually checked the bedrooms to the right. All the rooms had bathrooms, and all the fixtures were made of gold. This was an exquisite home.

"I had reached the last bedroom, opened the door, and started inside. The room was cool, colder than the rest of the house. I reached for the light switch, and a child-like voice said, 'Don't,' and a hand brushed across my hair and face. I backed out of the room, and the voice said, 'Please, don't go. Please come back.' I shut the door just as Tony and Mr. Patterson arrived. I must have looked pale, probably I was ashen-faced. Mr. Patterson laughed and said, 'I see you've met her.'

"'Yes,' I answered, 'I met someone. I think.' Tony and our guide opened the door, walked in, and put on the light. Of course, there was no one there. But the room was cold, even colder than when I first entered. Mr. Patterson explained that Miss Irene Crater waited many years for her best friend to come back home.

"'You see,' he said, 'Miss Crater was very shy. She didn't even dine with her brother or sister. She took all her meals in her room. In fact she barely left her room at all. Another thing,' continued Patterson, 'her friend was not known to her family, Willard or Jane. Many local folks said her friend was a ghost, a ghost who visited her the first night she lived here in the mansion and continued to visit every night until her death.'"

Hanging Rock

Back before the 1900s, there were places scattered about the Appalachian foothills where people didn't trust, nor did they depend on the county law officials to right any wrongs committed against them. They believed in taking care of their own problems and those of their family. Those were the ones most people didn't want to cross in any manner. In most cases, they were a close-knit group who didn't associate with anybody outside their own circle, and everybody else took special care to steer clear of the entire lot. Richard Dimsdale tells of such a group of people and their own special place called Hanging Rock.

"There was a huge granite cliff-like rock on the back side of my grandfather's property. As kids, me and some of my male cousins loved to explore the woods beyond the pasture. We were always finding arrowheads and other Indian stuff in the cave-like space under the rock. We could imagine all kinds of things happening there. It always was a mysterious place. We were allowed to roam free about the acreage in the daylight hours, but Grandpa would always want us away from the woods by sundown.

"'It's no place for folks, especially boys, to be when dark comes. It is full of evil spirits then. So you boys make sure you're at the house by dark,' he'd say. We all figured

Grandpa was just old and it was his way to keep us close to the house. For a few years, it worked. But then when I was about eight or nine years old, things changed. The family was visiting the grandparents one weekend. My cousins were there too, and as the day grew late, we ventured beyond the pasture into the woods and on to the hanging rock. We were hot and sweaty by the time we climbed up the granite-topped hill. A light wind blew and cooled us off as we waited for dark. We believed we were big then, big enough not to be treated like babies, and we would prove it to Grandpa by staying out till full dark. Besides, the oldest of us, Tommy, was about twelve, and he said there wasn't anything in the dark that wasn't there in the daylight. We all looked around and didn't see anything. I decided Tommy was right and lay back on the warm rock watching the day slide away into night.

"When it was full dark with stars shining in the sky and lightning bugs blinking all around us, we decided to head back to Grandpa's house. As we were coming back through the woods, it was really dark and staying on the path, probably made by animals, was hard. When we were about midway between the rock and the pasture, I heard something behind us. I looked back and saw an eerie glow of a light about eight or nine feet above the ground. There was nothing holding it up, yet it was coming closer to us. I yelled. The others looked back and saw the light, and we ran. We ran as fast as we could, and still the light came after us. When we broke through the black, dark woods into the pasture, I looked over my shoulder and saw the light at the tree line. It stayed. It didn't come beyond the woods. The closer we got to Grandpa's house, the more I knew he was right about evil spirits in the woods after dark. The light kept glowing. We were almost in the yard, and I had a paining stitch in my side from running so hard. I looked back again and saw the light was still there, glowing, then nothing. It disappeared.

Hanging Rock

"That night after we were all tucked into bed, Grandpa told us the story he'd heard all his life. Back before 1900, the farm property was owned by a family named Canner. They were known to be strange and mean. One night the Canner bunch kidnapped some men they were sure had cheated them, and the Canners held a mock trial. The men were convicted and sentenced then and there. Ropes were tied to a large tree limb that hung out over the rock. A noose was fashioned at the other end and pulled over the prisoners' necks, and then the Canners pushed the men off the rock to swing in the night until they were dead. That's how the place got its name. And that's why it was indeed haunted.

"The lights are believed to be the ghost of one of the men hanged all those many, many years ago. He is still trying to get away from the night-time trial at Hanging Rock. But for unknown reasons, he doesn't come beyond the woods. A lot of people have seen the light and heard the story. I have seen the light and heard the story of the Canners of Hanging Rock and believe it to be true. I cherish these old mountains and know this is the home of my heart. But sometimes as the sun is falling behind the high ridges, a shiver grabs me and I look over my shoulder. I know there are surely more places in these deep mountain woods that belong to the ghosts of the long dead, places where man once indeed carried out evil, places like Hanging Rock, where maybe the stories are not yet known."

The Baby's Cry

Seems a distant relative had a little baby that died at nine months old, but she never lived here in this house," says the woman brushing a wisp of silver-streaked brown hair away from her forehead. Laura Brooks sits on the sofa with her legs crossed. Then clasping her hands in her lap, she looks across the room as though seeing across the vastness of time. She blinks clear blue eyes, takes a deep breath, and continues in a soft voice. "It was only about six years ago, but somehow, it seems like a hundred years—or maybe just yesterday—that my house was haunted by a child."

Laura and her husband, Craig, had moved from the city to the rural north Georgia mountains, close to the North Carolina border. The town was small, the people friendly, and besides a great old farmhouse to live in, a small floral shop on the town's square was also for sale. A dream come true, thought the couple whose children were grown and retirement was at hand.

Laura clasps and unclasps her small hands and continues in her soft voice to tell her story. "We jumped at the chance to get the house even though it was a pretty bad mess. It had stood empty for almost five years. Vandals, I guess mostly teenage kids, had done a lot of damage. But this house had so many possibilities and it seemed just perfect for us, so we bought it. It was after we got everything cleaned up and had moved in that we heard rumors that some devil worshippers had held meetings and carried out rituals in this house. The police were always chasing intruders off. Anybody could get in through the ceiling opening on the carport and cross over through the attic crawlspace and come down in the back bedroom. Heavy, custom-made drapes were left on the windows and nobody could see inside, so I guess we'll never know for sure what went on here. But a child was surely somehow involved.

"We hadn't lived here long when I noticed things began to be missing—like the silverware and other things would be found in odd places—not where I had put them. It was when I started questioning these things being gone and others in the wrong places that I began to notice all the plants and flowers in the house were dying. It was then, too, I began to hear the child cry. The first time I heard it I really believed a baby was somehow in the house, but no one had heard the crying but me and there was no baby anywhere. I told Craig, my husband, after hearing the crying baby several times, that our house had a ghost. He thought I was just joking and didn't take me seriously. But he hadn't heard it either. It was rather eerie to hear a child, a baby, calling, 'Mama, Mama,' and only me hearing it. I mentioned to several people the cries and the things missing and moved. I even tried to discover whom the voice might have belonged to, wondering if perhaps it was some lost spirit somehow trapped in our house. Nobody knew anything.

"We had begun procedures to purchase the floral shop right after we moved in, and everything had gone through, so we now found ourselves in the florist business. It was exciting to know we owned our own business. We hired a couple of people, and after things got started and the business began to pick up, I just went in part-time to keep up on the paperwork and business end of things. Our employees had worked for the previous owner and really knew more about how to do things than I did. I liked this, and so did my husband as it didn't consume all our time, yet eventually would provide extra income. Owning and operating a floral shop, even in a small town, was a learning experience, and Craig and I both found it to be something we enjoyed sharing. We became more and more excited about retirement. Our own business, our own home in the mountains. Life was good, we thought, but we didn't know how the turn of events would affect us . . . maybe forever.

"One Sunday afternoon, Lisa, my daughter, and her family had come to visit. We were talking about the shop and the do's and don'ts of management and washing up the dinner dishes when the child cried, 'Mama, Mama.' Lisa dropped the dish cloth and hurried to the doorway of the den and looked in. Then, with a puzzled look on her face, she turned and walked back to the kitchen sink. 'Did you hear that baby crying?' she asked.

"'Yes,' I answered, continuing to dry the plates in the dish drainer. 'I've heard it lots of times. And you've heard it now, too. It's what I've been telling everybody about, and nobody has heard it but me—until now. I'm so glad somebody else has heard it.'

"'But where did it come from? Who was it?' she asked. 'I know it was a baby.'

"'I agree,' I said. 'But I don't know who it is, where it is, why it is here, why it stays, or why I have been the only one to hear it. Everybody thinks I'm crazy when I mention it, so I just don't say anything about it anymore. It's just a crying. It doesn't hurt anybody.'

"'Is there anything else?' Lisa asked, wiping off the sink for the third time.

"'No. Just some things are missing. The knives from the silverware and stuff gets moved around, but nothing bad. It's just unnerving to hear that baby cry and nobody else hear it,' I said. Lisa looked very concerned but didn't say anything else. The dishes were finished, so we joined the rest of the family in the den. They were watching a ball game on the television and wouldn't have heard a bomb going off. Lisa and her family left in the early evening. She didn't mention the crying baby until she called later in the week. I told her it was still there, but not to worry; it had been there longer than we had, and it wasn't hurting anyone physically.

"About two weeks later, Craig and I were in the den. It was a lazy Sunday afternoon. I was reading a book, and he was lying in the floor. He had been watching television, and the floor felt good to his back, which occasionally went out like everybody's our age. I guess he had gotten comfortable, or the program he was watching was boring, because he had dozed off to sleep. I didn't wake him. That's when the baby's crying sounded. 'Mama. Mama.' Craig came full awake and sat up.

"'Are the grandchildren here?' he asked. 'I thought I heard one of them calling mama.'

"'No, Dear,' I answered, 'just us.'

"'But I heard someone call mama,' he stated in a bewildered, sleepy tone of voice. 'I'm sure I heard it. Did you hear it?'

"'Yes, I heard it,' I said, closing my book. 'That's what I've been hearing for months. I'm so glad you finally heard it. Lisa heard it too when she was here.'

"'Well, we need to do something,' he said, crawling up on the couch. 'That's really strange.'

"'I agree,' I said, relieved I now had two witnesses to the crying.

"I spoke to several people, who wouldn't think I was crazy, about what needed to be done to remove the crying from our house. One said to call Ghost Busters. Someone else suggested we move, but a minister suggested we exorcise the ghost from our home and told me how it might be done. I talked with Craig, and he agreed. The crying baby had to go, and being Christian people, we believed we could do it.

41

Soon we were so busy with trying to do something about the ghost in the house that we didn't even pay attention to things that were happening at the shop. Now that I look back, maybe I should have wondered about a connection. The coolers were off many mornings, and the repairman was called. When the coolers were checked, no problem was ever found. Once I was sure I would have to replace them. Then the coolers would mysteriously begin working again. The repairman could never explain the strange goings-on concerning the on-and-off workings of the coolers.

"Then one early morning, a neighbor telephoned to inform us the shop was on fire. The firemen couldn't remember our last names but knew Mrs. Brown lived across the road from us and so made the call to her. Craig and I arrived to find our business only blackened timbers and ashes. Small flames still danced amid the cinders as firemen hosed water on the charred, smoking beams that now hung like my broken dreams. Townspeople tried to console us as we stood in the parking space in puddles of filthy water and watched the fire department gather their equipment and return it to the fire truck and drive slowly away. It hurt so bad I felt my heart would break. And I couldn't stop the tears that continued to trail down my soot-smudged face.

"Days later, the pain of loss was still raw and I wondered if it would ever go away. And while I tried to find a reason for the fire, the baby's cries still echoed through the rooms of my house. After several weeks, I decided I had to let the shop go and again concentrate on exorcising the ghost from my house. The shop was gone; the child's cries were not. Again I talked with the minister and prayed to God for guidance. I did as the man of God advised and began at the door's entrance most often used. With my hand, I made the sign of the cross over the doorpost and said, 'In the name of Jesus Christ, I command all evil spirits to leave this house. This house is washed with the blood of Jesus Christ.' I continued through the house and made the sign of the cross and repeated those words at every doorway entrance. From that day on, we've never heard sounds of the child crying in our home.

"Somewhere, I've heard it said that ghosts, spirits, or unearthly energy try to latch onto people or inanimate objects. I believe this is true and did indeed happen in our case. Craig bought a car at an auction. It appeared to be a good car. He brought it home and parked it in the carport. The next day it refused to crank. He called a mechanic to come and check it out. The mechanic found nothing wrong—no reason the car should not work. The mechanic left rather bewildered. I reasoned the car should work, but didn't. I began to wonder if by sitting in the carport, maybe the car was possessed. I went outside to the carport to where the useless car sat, and I exorcised it the same way I had exorcised the house. With the next turn of the ignition key, it cranked and never failed again.

"Later, Craig took some construction equipment from the barn to a job site where he was going to help build a small lake. Once there, the equipment refused to work. A mechanic repairman was called to the construction site and the machine was checked. No reason was found for the machine to refuse to run. My husband was puzzled. The man contracting the work was puzzled, and together they began to go over the machine for loose wiring or something—anything that might have been overlooked. Craig began to tell Mr. Philips, the contractor, of the strange happenings surrounding us. Mr. Philips, a godly man himself, suggested exorcising the equipment. Craig and Mr. Philips exorcised the construction equipment, and when finished, Craig climbed on it and it cranked right off.

"It has really been a very strange experience and one I'm not sure everyone would believe, but it's true, as true as night follows day. Our home is free from all evil now; we don't hear crying, nothing is missing anymore, everything is where it is supposed to be, and my inside plants and flowers are thriving. But the yard I didn't think about until just a few days ago when it was brought to my attention." Laura stood and gestured toward the door. Together, we stepped outside.

The yard was barren and brown. There was no grass at all, no flowers about the stoop. It was just ground, perhaps sick with something not quite understandable. She gazed sadly at the brown earth. "We've tried everything to get grass to grow, but it won't," Laura said. Then she sighed and looked to one of the big pine trees fronting the road. A large rip in the bark glistened as the afternoon sun's rays touched on the glob of resin beginning to melt and ooze down the tree trunk. "Lightning has struck that big tree there," she said, pointing to the pine tree, "three times."

Again Laura sighed, then she smiled her bright smile and said, "You know, I think I should exorcise the yard."

The Maiden Aunt

Back in olden times it seemed every southern Appalachian family had an old maid aunt. The Morgan family, back in the 1920s, was no exception. Aunt Lily Morgan was a tall, lovely woman. She had just never found the right man to share her life. Oh, several young blades had proposed, but she'd gently turned them down. Aunt Lily made herself useful; she babysat, baked, helped with weddings, births, and funerals. The Morgans didn't know what they would do without their dear Aunt Lily. Now, Lilly had a talent for seeing events that were going to happen. She'd be sitting at the dining room table and blurt out, "Margie's pregnant," or "Hank, I wouldn't take that job if I was you." At first no one in the family paid the slightest attention to their sweet aunt. But as time went by and Lily's statements were almost always right on the money, family members who ignored her warnings found out too late how right she was.

It was 1923, and Edward Morgan got a job driving a log truck. The pay was good, and in time he got his younger brother Samual a job as a logger's helper on the trucks. One night, as supper was ending, Edward was talking about the run he had the next day. It was down the mountain, across the bridge over the Coosawattee River, and on to the depot.

"Samual," said Aunt Lily, "I don't think you should go with Edward tomorrow."

"Why not?" asked Edward.

"Because," she answered, "if Samual goes on that truck tomorrow he could get hurt, bad hurt."

Edward, a smile on his face, asked, "What about me? Will I get hurt?"

"Oh no. You will be all right. It's Samual that I see trouble for," the woman stated.

Samual Morgan, despite being a teenager, was no fool. He flatly declared, even if he got fired, he was not going to work the next day. Aunt Lily too often was correct in her predictions.

The next day, Edward drove the logging truck down the mountain, and said aloud, "No trouble yet. Maybe Aunt Lily is wrong this time." He drove through the muddy streets and started across the wooden bridge over the Coosawattee River. He was dead center when the bridge began to sag and slowly collapse into the raging water below. Edward climbed out the truck window and swam to shore. He was cold and scared, but unhurt.

The sheriff and the sawmill owner arrived soon after and checked things out. "It's a good thing your brother wasn't with you, Edward," the sheriff said. "Look how the logs crushed the passenger side of the truck."

"Yes," said the mill owner. "He would have been crushed. Crushed to death, for sure."

After that episode no one in the Morgan family ever doubted Aunt Lily again.

*   *   *

It was March of 1926, and the Morgans were all in the parlor after supper. Edward and Samual were talking about trout fishing. Julie was knitting, Mama was pouring coffee, and Daddy was busy reading the local newspaper. Suddenly, Aunt Lily smiled, closed her eyes, and said, "Just listen to that beautiful music." The family all looked at one another because not a one had heard any music at all. They all waited for Lily to make a prediction, but she didn't. She just sat there, a little smile on her lovely face. At times she would say, "Oh, I wish you all could hear it. It is the most beautiful music I ever heard."

"Why can't we hear it?" asked Daddy. But no one answered him. Lily just sat there, her eyes closed. She swayed to music only she could hear. Suddenly, she stopped swaying, opened her eyes, and said, "Oh, that wonderful music just stopped."

And Aunt Lily, with a smile on her face, closed her eyes and died.

Ghosts in
Ole Virginny

Susan Thigpen, growing up in southwest Virginia, tells of some ghostly happenings. The house she and her family lived in was a pre-Civil War home in Wytheville County. The house was a large rambling structure with many acres and complete with a dirt basement for storage of home-canned goods and root vegetables.

"First off," relates Susan, "every night you could hear a herd of horses run up to the house, circle it, then run off around the barn. Of course, no one ever saw the herd of horses. But you could hear them neighing and snorting. And this went on all the while we lived in the old house. Another thing happened about five or six times a year. After the horses cantered off, we would see a young man. He was dressed in gray clothing, and he held his left arm, which was bleeding. Everyone who saw him over the thirty years we lived there thought he was a Confederate soldier who was lost in time. Many people saw the bleeding soldier and heard the horses, but no one has an explanation that isn't ghostly.

"Here is another odd fact about the house. There was a door from the front parlor to a hallway. At night the door would not stay closed. During the day, you could shut it, but at night it would just pop open. So every night Mother would put a heavy piece of furniture against it. And every morning the heavy furniture was moved and the door would be open.

"We did have a ghost in the house; about once a month an old woman would come and sit on my daughter Dorothy's bed. We knew nothing about the old woman, although an elderly woman lived and died in the house in the late nineteenth century. The old woman would just appear. She never said anything to Dorothy, but her breath was ice cold on Dorothy as she lay there waiting for the apparition to disappear as always. Today, Dorothy just laughs and says, 'After growing up with the old woman, I got used to her.'

"Another strange thing in our family was Mother. We never could surprise her at Christmas, Mother's Day, or her birthday. She could always predict what us kids got her for a present. We didn't know the full extent of how much she envisioned; she did not like the ability to know things when there wasn't any explanation for her knowing. Mother didn't tell us about the things she knew were going to happen. We thought she was afraid of the power she possessed.

"A dramatic event occurred, and it concerned a neighbor who lived across the road from us. One night, it was about 4 a.m., mother woke us all up. 'I had a dream,' she said. 'It was about our neighbor, Margie Milton.' Pacing the floor, she continued, 'It was a wild dream. Margie kept trying to get me to go somewhere with her.' Mother had slept uneasily all night, waking up, then falling back to sleep, only to have the dream start over again and again. When the entire family was up, Mother urged our father to go over and check on Margie Milton.

"'But it's four o'clock in the morning,' grumbled Dad. Still, he gave in and went across the road to the Milton place. He wasn't gone long, and when he returned, he had a strange look on his face. 'You kids go to bed,' he ordered.

'You got to go to school in a little while.' The next day at school we found out Margie Milton had hanged herself in the barn next to her house.

"My mother never ever predicted what presents we got her or told us her terrifying dreams again."

The Robinson Place

Houses in the southern Appalachian foothills have often seen infants birthed and the aged die and all of life in between. But sometimes spirits refuse to leave even should death come. Such are the tales surrounding the old Robinson homestead.

Young Bruce Beasley moved into the old two-story Robinson place shortly after the former residents, Mr. and Mrs. Robinson, had been found murdered inside the home. It was suspected that ne'er-do-wells in the area committed the crime with robbery as their motive, but it was never proved. Bruce had heard stories of strange noises and lights seen at the Robinson house, but the young man wasn't scared. He was twenty-three years old, had a job, and felt the need to be on his own. Besides, he was used to hearing tales of ghosts and haunted houses and rowdy spirits as his parents were what some called Natural Psychics and were often called on to check out strange, unusual, and unnatural occurrences.

After moving into his new home and getting everything in its place, Bruce noticed how bare the walls were and made a special trip into town to purchase some kind of wall decorations. He thought about the plates his mother had in her kitchen and the little shelf with the do-dads and framed pictures in the living room. These things reflected his parents. He'd find just the right thing to reflect his own self and then the place would feel more like his home, he thought as he drove his old truck on the narrow, winding road into town. The Prestons had a selection of pictures in the back of their general store in the hardware/housewares section. He had seen them stacked against the wall for a couple of years.

Two hours later, Bruce returned to his new home with a large picture of a ship on the open ocean. He had never seen an ocean or a ship, but he thought it looked adventurous and he knew he was surely that. He also had two small pictures of wild ducks. Bruce was a mountain man. He had hunted nearly all his life and loved the outdoors. The bright-colored leaves of autumn in the background showed nature at its finest and made the pictures really stand out in their dark wooden frames. Bruce had been unable to pass up the small wooden crosses. They reminded him of his old granny who had died during his teenage years. She had had crosses hung in every room of her rickety old house. When he had asked why she had so many, she had laughed and told him they held her house up. He smiled, remembering the old woman and how she had spoiled him rotten in his early childhood.

Bruce hung his pictures and the crosses in appropriate places. He then ate something for supper and went to bed. The next day, when he returned home from work, the pictures in the living room were askew and one of the crosses lay on the floor—broken. He thought he hadn't hung the pictures straight and that's why they were crooked, and perhaps he hadn't gotten the nail in good enough to hold the cross and it had just slipped off. He liked the cross where it was and figured he'd get another one come payday and use a bigger nail to put it up with.

Later in the night he was brought instantly awake by the sound of someone coming up the stairs. Remembering the former residents had been murdered, Bruce reached into the drawer of his bedside table and got out his pistol. When he slipped through the darkness to check on the intruder, there was no one to be found.

A few days later Bruce came home from work literally exhausted. His back hurt from moving heavy boxes filled with machine parts, and his head ached from the loud noise of the saws. Bruce got himself a beer from the refrigerator and sat down to rest and watch the news on the television. He thought about how hard his job at the saw mill was, but it had afforded him a place of his own, a television, and maybe, he thought, if he could keep getting overtime, a better truck in the next year. Bruce reached for his beer sitting on the chair's side table. He was stunned—all the words on the beer can's label were spelled backward. He blinked his eyes. The television began to go on and off. After a couple of minutes, Bruce saw the label on the beer can was right and the television was working properly. "Must be ghosts," he muttered, guzzling the remainder of the beer. All was quiet for the rest of the night.

Later in the week, Bruce came home to find all his phonograph records strewn about the floor and the television blaring. That night the water faucets kept turning themselves on. Bruce would turn them off, and soon they would be back on—open full force with water gushing from the spigots. Finally, after maybe two hours or more of this craziness, Bruce went outside and turned off the water main to the house. Again he mumbled about ghosts and their uncalled-for antics. He thought maybe he'd see if his parents could come and get rid of them. He didn't have time to deal with this haunting stuff. He wanted to invite Ellen Ann Crawford over some night to see his place, but he didn't want her scared off. He really liked the tall red-headed woman with all her freckles.

The next night it was after dark when Bruce came home. The porch light was blinking on and off. As soon as the man got out of his old truck, he proceeded up onto the porch and jerked the fixture down. Wires hung haphazardly. Using black electrical tape, Bruce taped them up and went inside as if he did this every day. Again, the young man got a beer, sat in his chair and watched the television. Suddenly the beer was snatched from his hand and turned upside down. Tired from his day's work and whatever was aggravating him, Bruce growled, "I have $150 in my pocket, so I'll buy all the beer I want." Nothing else happened . . . that night.

A few days later, Bruce remembered things his parents did to "remove spirits from this world." He decided he'd try one of the things he had heard his parents speak of. Maybe the ghost or whatever it was would pack up and leave. He put the Bible, opened, on the small table that he had centered in the living room. He then proceeded to hang crosses on three of the walls. He went to bed wondering what the morning would bring. But it didn't take till morning to get results. Bruce was awakened in the middle of the night by awful noises coming from the living room. He hurriedly stumbled through the dark to investigate. By the time he reached the living room, all was quiet, yet the Bible was turned over and the crosses all hung upside down. Bruce didn't touch anything, just went back to bed.

The next night, after he had righted everything in the living room, he sat down at the kitchen table to eat supper. As he reached for his silverware, the steak knife and fork flipped up and up in the air and came back down to stick up in the tabletop. "This is too, too much," Bruce yelled. "Get out of here, cause I ain't. I'm staying." Before the echo of Bruce's words died away, a voice deep and gravelly, in somewhat of a hurt tone, replied, "Okay. You want to play that way?" Bruce had had enough. Now the ghost was getting nasty and maybe even threatening him. Since Bruce couldn't see what had spoken and the room instantly became icy cold, he jumped up from his chair and crashed out through the nearest window. Glass flew in all directions as he landed in a run and frantically made for a neighbor's house.

The young man refused to go back to that house and asked the neighbor to go and get his truck. He left everything in the house and never did get anything out. To this very day, Bruce Beasley refuses to drive down the road where the house stood empty for many years before falling in on itself, he hopes taking the haunting spirit down with it.

Keepers of the Earth

It is believed, here in the Appalachian foothills, that certain folks have been given assignments by spirits of the long-dead Native American ancestors to watch over the earth. They are called "Keepers of the Earth" and "Caretakers of the Mountains." The people selected simply can't *not* do it. It was predestined long before their birth that they be the chosen ones. Some, not even born or raised in these rural southern mountains, are somehow called here when responsible majority is reached, and sometimes through mysterious experiences, they learn of their calling and follow the teachings of the long dead—the spirits who entrust our good earth to their careful tending.

Such was the discovery of Joan Smith, a young woman born in Patterson, New Jersey, and raised near Ashville, North Carolina. When she was twenty-three years old, she married and moved to Atlanta, Georgia. Her husband died after two years of marriage, and Joan was drawn north to the mountains of north Georgia. She couldn't explain her desire to live there, but somehow she knew it was her true home. She searched for months before she found the old farm for sale. It was in sad shape, needing much work, but it was the place she had been called to. Joan lived in a tent while the house repairs were being made. She walked the width and breadth of the land, and it spoke to her. The bogs, the virgin timber, the streams, and rocky hillsides called out their needs, and she knew in her heart these things she would see to.

"The spirits of the earth, they speak to me," she says in a shaky tone, as tears slide from her eyes. In a voice as sincere as an old mountain hymn, she continues, "They summoned me from another lifestyle not only to protect the historical relics of the past found on this land, but to preserve them, so there will be a tomorrow here when it is someone else's turn to take over and do the tending.

"It's a strangeness to know and feel the past of your surroundings, to feel the joys and sufferings of those who lived here many generations before, the worst sorrows coming from the cold spots where the wind blows the tops of the trees continuously. Yet contentment comes from knowing I am indeed where I am supposed to be and fulfilling my destiny to be a caretaker of these mountains, a keeper of the earth, as was destined long before my time."

The Mine at Plant #5

The Appalachian mountain chain is dotted with mines from one end to the other. They are host to a variety of earthly treasures. The southernmost foothills of the chain have birthed gold, copper, coal, marble, talc, and a multitude of other minerals both desired and demanded by man. The mining industry has been seen as good for the economy, for when mines were dug and opened, those gouged holes in the earth created jobs, built towns, and raised hopes for many when there was little else.

Removal of the treasures from deep underground has always been a grueling task, and many workers went for long months—even years—without ever seeing the light of day, going to their jobs before sunup and not returning home until after sundown, seven days a week. Yes, treasures were there, deep under the ground, and man has taken them without realizing sometimes the earth demands payment. Over the years, many have lost life and limb as payment for harvesting the bounty of the earth's core.

Haunting stories have been told down through the years about southern Appalachian foothill mines and the men who worked them. These stories cry out to be heard, many perhaps as warnings to those who still make their wage in the dark of deep tunnels far from the light of day. Or maybe these haunting tales simply cry to be heard lest they be forgotten with the passage of time. One mine in the Georgia mountains believed to be cursed or haunted is called The Cavern and is adjacent to Plant #5. In the past twenty or so years, there have been seven deaths in that place.

Native Americans once roamed this land and were careful with the earth to maintain a balance between man and Mother Earth. If they took something, they gave something in return. Before their removal to Oklahoma on the Trail of Tears, they spoke of cloud spirits that watched over the earth and her treasures, demanding payment when the earth balance cried out from pain. Clara Anderson, wife of one of the workers at the mine, tells of seeing one of these cloud spirits.

Clara's husband, Boyd, had been a worker at the mine for more than twenty years. He worked the night shift. One night he was running late and, in his haste, forgot his lunch. Clara soon discovered the lunch pail containing the sandwiches and thermos of coffee on the kitchen table and decided she and her son would take the lunch to the mine and give it to the night foreman in hopes he would see to it that her husband received it before the lunch whistle blew at 2 A.M. The shift foreman didn't generally go down into the mines but remained topside in the little office house close to the main gate.

With her young son in the passenger's seat of the car, holding the lunch pail, Clara drove down the narrow road leading to the mine. The weather was warm for the time of year, and they rode with the car windows down. It was obvious a storm was brewing, for the night was sooty black—no stars or moon shown anywhere overhead. As they got closer to their destination, a heaviness in the air began to settle and even filled the car with a weighty unease. Clara and her twelve-year-old son, Bobby, talked about school and his friends and the upcoming holidays. The woman felt an unexplained eeriness but didn't want to frighten the boy.

Yet she could see the tension building in him. Topping the rise in the road and crossing the railroad tracks, they saw a green, fog-thick cloud. It hovered and twisted like a shroud or spirit over the entire valley below, the place known as The Cavern and Plant #5.

*   *   *

There is a place deep in the tunnels at the mine of Plant #5 that even the biggest, toughest, or longest seasoned miners fear. Near the entrance to the dark tunnel leading long and deep into the earth, one can hear the tap-tap-tapping of someone chipping away deep in the dark. The strangeness of this is that this particular tunnel has been closed off for decades because many years ago a young man was crushed to death as he worked. It is believed by many of the miners that the tap-tap-tapping is coming from the spirit of the young miner who is perhaps still chipping away at the tunnel wall, still on the job all these long years after his death.

*   *   *

A mineworker named Leroy and a coworker named Thomas were doing some work on a dozer deep inside the mine. Such work was common; the machines were big and heavy, and it often took more time to move them topside than the repairs themselves required. The work on the dozer had been long, tedious, and tiresome. When the mechanics came to a stopping place, they took a break from their work to rest and stretch the kinks from their bodies.

As Leroy and Thomas leaned against the big blade at the front of the dozer, discussing what was left to be done, they turned to see someone walking in their direction. Even at a distance they could see he was young and dressed in clothes of another era. His boots were not like any they had seen in many years. And the man carried a tin lunch bucket. Leroy and Thomas figured it was maybe someone new to the job. Having rested, they returned to the dozer.

60

Once the machine was fixed and they'd returned to the main crew, Leroy asked his boss who the young man was. The boss said there wasn't anyone new on the job. Nobody had been hired.

Leroy and Thomas had both seen the man and described him and his clothes to the boss. An employee himself for almost thirty years, their boss suddenly got a strange look on his face and said that they had just described, in detail, a young man who had been crushed to death by a long screw back in early 1970.

*   *   *

Joe Richards, another equipment mechanic, tells another haunting story that took place in the tunnels of the mine at Plant #5.

Joe was well into his workday, working on a dump truck. Frank, a coworker and friend, was running a dozer nearby. Each man was concentrating on the job before him. Suddenly, the dozer hit the tunnel wall. Frank turned the engine off and climbed down to check for damage as some of the earthen side of the wall had crumbled down. Joe had noticed the dozer was silent and seen Frank climb down. He stopped what he was doing on the dump truck and went to see if Frank needed help. Joe and Frank discovered that the wall the dozer had hit was thin with a cavern-like room behind it. The wall separating the cavern room and the tunnel was now just rubble on the dozer's big blade. When the falling earth settled, the two men looked closer into the hole and saw graves inside with crosses at the end of each earthen mound. As the two men stood puzzled and staring at the graves with the cross markers, the dozer cranked up.

Frank yelled, yet stood frozen in fear. Joe ran to the dozer, climbed up on it, and shut off the fuel valve, thinking that would turn the machine off. But the dozer kept on running, and it was moving—in the direction of the cavern, the graves, and Frank.

"Run! Run!" Joe shouted to Frank, knowing there was nothing else to do. Frank, jolted out of his trance-like state by Joe's voice, stumbled and ran from the dozer's path. Only one thought was in the minds of the men: to get away—far away—and they ran, but not before seeing the dozer swallowed up by the secret cavern with the cross-marked graves. The surrounding tunnel wall came crashing down to bury once again what had been kept secret for a countless measure of time.

The Cat

Many young men living in the mountain foothills of the Appalachian chain were drafted into the military during the 1960s to serve in Vietnam. Many others joined willingly to serve their country. Andrea, a small woman with curly brown hair, delicate features, and a soft voice, tells a strange and unusual story surrounding her brother's two-tour military duty in the Asian jungle.

The family's three-generation house was located on the outskirts of town. There were no family pets, as the mother and grandmother did not particularly like animals and definitely would never allow them inside the house. The day Andrea's brother, Bob, was scheduled to ship out for Vietnam, a large, gray, longhaired tomcat appeared at their home. It was first discovered at the dinner table, sitting in Bob's chair. The cat was immediately ousted from the house, and all the doors and windows were checked to make sure there was no way the stranger cat could make another secret entrance. Everything was closed up tight as a drum; not even a crack could be found. Later, as darkness fell and it came time for the family to retire for the day, the cat was once again found nested in a sleeping ball on the soldier brother's bed. He was once more put out and told to stay out! The house was again checked for any openings;

even the basement and attic were searched for places the cat could have come inside. Again, none was found.

The cat was never fed or encouraged in any way to stay, yet stay it did. It was always discovered in the brother's places—his room, his chair, his bed. The family was disturbed time after time to put the strange cat with its yellow eyes and black padded feet out the door and almost upon turning around to find him back, watching the family from spaces Bob always filled. This went on for as long as Bob was away. But on the very day Bob arrived home from his second tour of duty, not to leave again, the strange cat disappeared and has never been seen again.

Footsteps

Patricia Ryan's mother was very sick. But she was released from the local hospital and went to Patricia's home. She lay in a hospital bed in her daughter's bedroom. Patricia's niece, Cathy, came on Saturday to help out and to give Patricia moral support. It was about midnight when they checked Patricia's mother, whom they called Granny, making sure the bed rails were up and the door left open. Cathy took the living room couch, while Patricia slept in a recliner. Both could hear Granny if she called or there were any unusual noises.

The next morning Patricia went into the kitchen to make breakfast. Cathy entered the kitchen, got a cup of coffee, and asked, "Aunt Patricia, did you hear anything last night?"

"No, I didn't. Why do you ask?"

"I heard someone walking in Granny's room," Cathy said. "The footsteps walked around Granny's bed, then came back to the foot of the bed. Aunt Patricia, I thought Granny had managed to get the hospital bed rails down and had gotten up. As sick and weak as she is, I thought that if she was up, she'd surely fall."

"I didn't hear anything," said Patricia. "I wonder what happened. You should have woke me up."

"I was going to, but you were exhausted; you needed

to sleep. So I went into Granny's room, and she was sound asleep. The bed rails were up, and everything was just as we left it."

The next Saturday, Cathy came again to Patricia's house. Granny's condition had gotten worse, and once again when night came, Patricia lay back in the recliner while Cathy stretched out on the couch. On Sunday morning, Cathy said, "Oh, Aunt Patricia, I heard the footsteps again, and this time they walked around the bed, then came down the hallway toward the parlor. I jumped up and went toward where the footsteps were coming from, and then they were gone. I didn't hear or see anything the rest of the night."

On Thursday night, Patricia's daughter, Sandy, came along with Patricia's sister, Adele, to stay with the old woman, for Granny's condition had worsened. Patricia slept in the parlor on the recliner, Adele on the sofa, and Sandy in the little bedroom down the hall. Sandy read a book well into the night. The next morning Adele and Patricia were in the kitchen when Sandy told what had happened during the night.

"I was reading when I heard someone walking around in Granny's room. The footsteps walked around Granny's bed, then crossed the hall and went into the bathroom."

"Who was it?" asked Adele.

"I thought it was you or Mama," said Sandy. "But I didn't hear any water running, and no one ever came out. I got up and went into the parlor. Both of you were fast asleep. I went down the hall to the bathroom, knocked on the door, and then opened it. There wasn't anybody in there. I don't know what it was or why I couldn't find anything. I know I didn't imagine it because I wasn't asleep. I feel like something strange is going on in this house."

Patricia also wondered if something strange was there. Something or someone was making a sound, yet nothing had been seen. The sound of footsteps continued to be heard in the night as long as the old woman lived.

Squeaking Gate

When the doctors gave up all hope for Milly Reagan's grandmother, the family brought her home to Milly's house. Grandma was comfortable and in no pain, and since she was in her eighties, the family thought it wouldn't be too long. Family members stayed with their ailing grandmother around the clock, as was normal for folks in the southern Appalachian mountains of Georgia. Gradually, though, her condition didn't change for better or worse. Milly said she'd take care of all Grandma's needs. Some of the family, those who lived close by, still dropped in to see their dear granny and show their love for her.

After about three weeks, life became routine. In late afternoon, Milly would leave her grandmother's side to telephone family members and inform them of her condition. One afternoon, about four o'clock, Milly was talking to her Aunt Irene on the telephone when she heard a knock at the front door. "Excuse me, Aunt Irene. Someone's at the door." Milly opened the door, but no one was there.

"Irene," said Milly, "there wasn't anybody there. I should have known that, because I didn't hear the gate squeak." Now in a lot of older homes in southern Appalachia, mountain folks have a porch and across the top of the steps is a gate. Not to keep folks out, but to keep grandchildren and other little ones from falling off the porch or down the steps.

"Darn," said Milly. "There's another knock on the door. Whoever it is, is hammering it good." Again Milly went to the door, and again no one was there. Milly went back and finished her conversation with Aunt Irene. She had just poured herself a cup of coffee when once again she heard the sound of persistent knocking on the front. Putting down her cup of coffee, she rushed to the door and flung it open. Nothing, no one. Something is wrong here, thought Milly as she went to check on her grandmother. Granny was lying there, but suddenly her eyes grew wide and she softly said, "I'm glad you finally came. I thought you'd be here sooner." Then she closed her eyes for the last time.

Milly raced to the phone, called the doctor, and had just hung up when she heard the gate on the porch open with its usual squeaking sound. She opened the door, but no one was there. The gate was open and still moving—but outward, not inward. Someone or something had just walked off of the porch. "I don't understand it," said Milly later, "but I don't think Granny's last words were to me, but to whoever it was that came and took her away."

Mountain Spirits

These hills and mountains are filled with history of the Native Americans, for these lands were once occupied by the Cherokee Nation. Sometimes folks tell strange stories about the spirits of these long-ago inhabitants appearing to them in one form or another. Jane Allen tells of spirits abounding on her land—land that had once belonged to her father but long before had belonged only to the earth and was inhabited by the old ones, the Cherokee.

Jane's chestnut hair catches the sun's late summer rays and glints auburn as she sits on her deck overlooking the Cohutta mountain range of the southern Appalachian chain and tells her story.

"I've always loved this place," she says, smiling. "I played here as a child even though the spring always felt eerie and the hollows were so dark it was always like night. We didn't live here. My family lived over in the next hollow, across the ridge. Daddy always rented out the little four-room house that was there in the cove." Jane points to a place unseen in a cluster of tall trees backed against a mountain to the east. There could have been a house there as she told the story, but everything was covered in kudzu and other wild climbing vines and the growing greenness left to the wilds of nature. Jane pauses, staring at the place as she points, as if trying to see some kind of picture in her mind. Then she continues.

"A lot of times folks didn't have the money to pay the rent, but Daddy never made anybody leave because they couldn't pay. He said times were hard and it was better to have somebody living there in the house than have it standing empty. He said a house with people living in it wouldn't fall down as long as it was needed to shelter someone. I guess it's so. When I grew up and married Cade, we moved to the little house when the people living there moved out. Sometimes folks wouldn't stay there long, said it was like the place was lonely or sad, being at the end of the dirt road and so dark there deep in that cove. And it was. Not like we are here on this ridge. But me and Cade made it home, and being newlyweds and times being hard, we were just proud we had a place of our own.

"We'd lived there about a month when we noticed the lights. They moved through the hollow. Then shortly after that we'd hear things—noises in the night. But when we'd get up out of bed to see what they were, we couldn't find anything. It was something. I could feel it. It watched us, and when we'd come home after dark, I'd always run from the car to the porch. It scared me. Daddy always said there were Cherokee graves on the hillside above the spring. And he believed spirits watched over their burial grounds for all time, saying they were the sentinels of the earth. I never knew if there were really any graves over there or not for sure.

"We lived in the little house for several years before we moved to the south side of the county. I said when we left that dark place, I'd never come back here. But the orchards had to be tended, and me and Cade had to help, and somehow the place—the land—seemed to beckon me and I'd get lonesome for it even though it still scared me at times. Sometimes me and Cade would just come and sit here on this ridge and watch the sun go down. I knew—spirits, ghosts, or no—this land had some kind of hold on me.

"Years passed and we finally had kids. Daddy got old and sick. The orchard fell to ruin and the house stood empty, and it was just like overnight it all went back to the wild—to nature. When Daddy died, he left the place to his kids. We all needed the money, so we sold it, but I made sure this plot of land didn't go. Part of me was bound to this land, and up here it was good spirits I felt. It's so high up, you can nearly touch the sky." Jane sighs, as she appears to drink in her surroundings. "The spirits don't scare me now. They give me a kind of comfort, and I feel protected by them. I guess maybe we've grown used to one another over time. They speak to me on the wind and in my dreams. Like last night." Jane brushes a wisp of hair, teased by a breeze, away from her face and smiles as she continues.

"I heard a sound in the night, a high-pitched noise, and I could see a light, like a flame. The noise grew louder and louder, and it woke me up. Even then I could still hear it and wondered where it was. But before I could find where it came from, it stopped and I went back to sleep. I didn't think about it any more until this afternoon when I was in Mama's room, seeing to her medicine, and I heard it again. But when I heard it then, I was wide-awake. 'I've got to see what that noise is,' I told Mama, taking the glass of water from her hand. 'I heard the same noise in the middle of the night last night, and it stopped before I could find it.'

"Mama nodded, and I hurried through the house to find fire in the utility room and the smoke and fire detector's high-pitched noise screaming out its warning. Flames licked up the wall. I had lit one of those little scented candles before going to see about Mama, but it was too close to the wall and had caught fire and, in its fury, was going wild. I grabbed a bucket of mop water and doused the blaze. The room was thick with smoke, and the alarm still sounded. As I opened the doors and turned on the fan, the smoke and fire detector shut off. I trembled inside and out as it echoed in my mind and I faced the charred black wall. I had heard the smoke and fire detector's warning the night before when there was no fire. I wondered if maybe the spirits were letting me know, ahead of time, of a sound I should be listening for."

The House
of the Gnome

Alvin Dunlap, now living in Chatsworth, Georgia, relates the eerie events that took place in a house he lived in. Back in the 1950s, Alvin, his brother, Arnold, and their parents moved into a large rambling house in Murphy, North Carolina. There was no horrific history to the three-story structure; it was just a house.

The Dunlaps had lived in the house about a month when Alvin and Arnold heard laughter out in the hallway. They didn't think much about it as they climbed into their beds. Then they heard a loud knocking at the bedroom door followed by more loud laughter. The laughter sounded as if it were coming from a young person. Both teenagers rushed into the hallway, bent on nabbing the jokester. No one was there. The next night the same thing happened, only this time they could hear soft footsteps going up the stairs to the third floor. They breathlessly followed, and when they arrived at the top of the house, nothing was there. The boys told their parents about their strange experience. Dad just laughed and said, "There are no such things as creatures in the night."

Two weeks later Alvin was listening to records in the

front room. All was quiet. Arnold and a friend were back of the house. A narrow hallway ran the length of the house, and to the left was a small bathroom. Alvin had just changed a record when Arnold and his friend came tearing down the hallway screaming like banshees.

"Alvin," shouted both boys, "there's a creature in the bathroom. It's, it's a gargoyle!"

"Yeah, sure," laughed Alvin. "And I'm the bogey man." So Alvin, laughing to himself, went down the long hallway. He didn't see anything at first in the dimly lit hallway. But reaching the end of the hall, Alvin stopped. He heard a laugh, then opened the bathroom door. He didn't see anything until he looked down. That's when the breath rushed out of his body. He wanted to run, but he couldn't. He was paralyzed. His hair stood straight up on end. For what he saw was a small creature about two-and-a-half feet tall with long arms and a gruesome looking face. The creature laughed and ran out the bathroom door. Alvin was too scared to follow it.

Daddy, who worked long hours at the sawmill, just laughed when he was told the strange tale. "I don't believe a word of it. And if it did happen as you boys say, it's one of your friends playing a joke on you."

The boys didn't see the little gnome during the summer months, but they still heard the childish laughter and the knocks on their bedroom door. One autumn evening, the boys were across the street sitting on Joe Stamey's front porch. Alvin, Arnold, Joe, and Harry Reid were comparing their BB guns. Alvin's father was at work, and his mother was attending a quilting bee. Arnold had left the dining room light on. As the boys bragged about their air guns, Harry gasped and pointed across the street.

"Look," he shouted, "it's that little thing again and it's jumping around on your dining room table."

"Let's get him," yelled Alvin, figuring there would be safety in numbers. Carrying their BB guns, the four rushed across the street and into the Dunlap house. There was nothing to be seen when they arrived, no one around but them.

"I'm telling you," said Joe, "if I get that thing in the sights of my gun here, you won't have to worry about him anymore." The teenagers went back to Joe's front porch. Alvin later said, "I wasn't too sure I wanted to meet that little gnome, or imp, whatever it was. I just wished my father could see it. I thought if he could see it, we might move out of that house. I had noticed Arnold was always scared, always looking over his shoulder to see if anything was there."

"There he is again," yelled Arnold. This time the boys snuck up to the lighted dining room. And there it was, a little gnome-like creature, laughing and jumping on the dining room table. They crept into the house, went across the dark hallway, and Alvin flung open the dining room door. They rushed in and once again saw nothing, but they all heard the laughter.

Two weeks later, about ten in the morning, the boys were in school, and Mother was out shopping. Dad, who had worked a double shift, was just getting home.

"I went into the kitchen," said Mr. Dunlap, "and heated up some coffee. I was going to drink it and go right to bed. I was pretty tired. I finished my coffee and went upstairs to my bedroom. Well, I'll tell you, I got pretty scared. When I got to the top of the stairs, I saw my bedroom door was open. I couldn't believe it, but this little gnome-like creature popped out, looked at me, laughed, and scampered away. There was no way I was going to chase it. It had the longest arms I ever saw. Besides, I was so scared I didn't know anything else. I now believed Alvin and Arnold's stories." One week later the Dunlaps moved away from the gnome house.

Forty years later, Alvin, on business in western North Carolina, decided to go to his old hometown. "I went to Murphy," said Alvin Dunlap, "to see if the old house was still there. The old neighborhood hadn't changed too much, and as I walked down the street, I expected to see the old rambling house gone. It wasn't. It looked exactly the same as the day we left it forty years ago. There was an old man sitting on the front stoop as I walked in front of my old house.

"Does anyone live here?" I asked the old man.

He grinned at me and said, "No. Ain't been nobody lived here for a spell. I'll tell you, son, this place is cursed, or something. Folks just don't live in this house for very long." Alvin thanked the man and thought, I'm going and I'm not really sure I want to know any more about what we called the gnome.

Premonitions
in the Night

The young man, born in Gilmer County, Georgia, was really a mountain boy. He lived there until near grown, working on the family apple farm. But as it is with mountain folk, sometimes the young leave home to better their education or find jobs. Chris Warren, the youngest child of four, went away to school. His aunt lived in Florida with a wonderful school nearby; Chris went to live with her. It was a different kind of place than the young man was used to. Flat land. Sand rather than red clay soil. Palm trees rather than one-hundred-year-old oak and pine trees whispering in breezes atop mountains as old as time itself. Chris tried to adjust to the climate and lifestyle, but he was a mountain boy through to his soul.

He went to school during the day and occasionally took on odd jobs in the evenings. But his nights were filled with home. He dreamed of rivers and streams, clean and clear, cold and sweet, and brimming with rainbow trout. He dreamed of the mountains with deer, squirrels, bobcats, and even bear roaming the lush forest. He dreamed of family, laughing and working on the farm, their labors hard but ever true to the dedication given to the land and its bounty.

It was in this dream state that Chris knew terror—terror

associated with the treasured mountain land. He awoke drenched in sweat, screams taking his breath away. He trembled with panic unlike any he'd ever known before. It was still dark of night, and Chris knew his family was sleeping, but he also knew that Don, his brother, was scheduled to spray the orchards in the early morning dawn before the wind arose. The big tractor was where the problem lay, and Chris realized he had to warn Don before he left the house, had to prevent the accident that would surely take his brother's life. The telephone rang on and on in the darkness before it was answered.

"Hello," came a sleepy answer on the other end of the telephone line.

"Don, Don," Chris said anxiously. "Don't get on the tractor. There's something wrong with it. Promise me you won't use it till it's checked out!"

"Okay. But it's the middle of the night now. Go back to sleep. I'm not going to see about it now," came the muffled voice.

"Okay—just promise, Don," Chris begged.

"I promise," Don growled and hung up the phone.

As dawn birthed on the night sky, Don made his way to the barn to begin a day of spraying the hillside orchards. Once inside the barn, facing the giant machinery, flickers of Chris' phone call—his warning to check the tractor— tumbled across his mind like a sleep-fogged dream. When Don checked the tractor tires, Chris' words chilled his blood. The back left tire had only two lug nuts holding it on the axle, and they were both loose. Had Don not been warned by his brother's premonition from nearly a thousand miles away and had he not heeded those words, an accident would have occurred, perhaps one that would have taken his life there on the steep orchard hillsides.

Chris often has premonitions, but none has ever preyed as heavy on his mind nor has any ever been more precise.

Birthday Ghost

Margery Stevenson lives on the Georgia–Tennessee border near Chattanooga. She has had some eerie events happen to her and her family. Here she tells of a birthday party that went beyond the realm.

Margery's husband, William, passed away thirteen years ago. "He was great with the family, and the grandchildren were oh-so-special to him. He always insisted every one of the children have a birthday party, a big birthday party. Sometimes William would scrimp and save just so the kids could have the party they wouldn't forget. This practice carried over to the grandchildren, and if possible, the parties became even bigger.

"William was a churchgoer, but one thing he insisted on was another world, a world parallel to ours. He thought some day man could, or would, go back and forth between the two worlds. He would laugh and say, 'Margery, here we sit watching television in our living room, and there could be a train roaring through and we would never know it.' William never told anyone of his idea of a parallel world except Margery. After William died, the kids grew up and, now with a passel of kids of their own, continued the birthday parties. Seems there was one every other week.

"William always said, 'If it's possible, Margery, I'll

come back for one more birthday party.' Well, William's been gone for thirteen years, and just before Christmas, there was a birthday party for the four-year-old great-grandson. Oh, how my son, as he held his grandson in his lap, wished that his dear father could be there for that party," said Margery.

"Anyway," she continued, "my son took pictures of all the grownups and of course the children. He said he'd get the film developed and give everyone a set of pictures."

Two weeks later, the son stopped by his mother's house. He said, "I got the pictures from the party. Here, Mama, are yours." She noticed her son was, well, a little disturbed. "Is something the matter, son?"

"Just look at the pictures, Mama."

"I did, and they all came out wonderful. All of us were there in all our finery. Now what's the matter, son?" Margery asked.

"You saw the pictures, right, Mama?"

"Yes," she answered.

"Look at this one," said her son in a strange voice. Margery did, and the picture he showed her was of her dear departed husband, William. He was standing in back of the birthday cake she had baked just two weeks ago.

Margery was stunned. "Where did you get this picture?" she asked.

"Mama, it was developed along with the rest of the pictures. Mama, look at the cake, the decorations; Papa was here. We didn't see him, but he was here. It's right on the film." The picture was put in a safe deposit box so it would be safe and wouldn't fade. It has been taken out only once, and that was for this book.

Where's Johnny?

Martin Kroll's father passed away in December 1947; Martin was born the following July. It was tough going for Martin's mother. During his early years, she was hospitalized many times. So Martin was shuttled between relatives in West Virginia and later in southwest Virginia.

In 1957 nine-year-old Martin was living with his father's sister and her husband. They lived in a three-room company house, one bedroom upstairs, and downstairs a living room and kitchen. Another aunt, Sophia, lived nearby. Martin's uncle had made a basketball hoop out of an old clothes hanger and hung it in the kitchen. The boy's basketball was a bunch of old socks rolled up into a ball. Aunt Sophia's son, Johnny, came to see his mother and the rest of the family. The young man drove a new 1957 Dodge Cornet. Johnny stayed about a week visiting all the folks, then left, driving his new Dodge back to Ohio.

That evening after Johnny left, Martin was shooting baskets in the kitchen with his rolled-up socks. His uncle sat at the kitchen table reading the newspaper. It was just before darkness fell. There was a back porch on the company house and an outside door. In the summer, Martin's uncle put a screen in the door. In colder weather, he would seal the door with a sheet of clear plastic to keep out the cold winter wind. Martin's uncle also put a latch on the top of the door so Martin couldn't go out when he wasn't supposed to. Martin had just sunk a basket when a knock was heard at the back door.

"Who is it?" asked both Martin and his uncle at the same time.

"Johnny," came the answer. They both went to the door and could see Johnny standing there. The uncle unlatched the door and pushed it open, but no one was there. Johnny had disappeared.

When Martin and his uncle told the aunt, she immediately called her sister, Sophia. Aunt Sophia said Johnny had left hours ago but that she would call Ohio the next day. She called friends in Columbus the next day, but no one there had seen Johnny. She called again the second day, and there was still no sign of Johnny. After talking it over with the family, Sophia called the police. The police in southwestern Virginia checked but came up with no hint as to what had happened to the young man. Then, several days later, the police discovered Johnny's car in a reservoir. Johnny's body was in the car. It was estimated that the time of his death was about the same time Martin and his uncle saw and heard Johnny at the back door.

Through the years, Martin visited his ailing mother every two weeks or so. In 1966, he joined the Army, and he and his mother wrote letters to one another all the time he was in service. When discharged, Martin got a job in southwest Virginia; he was there three months before being transferred to Lafollette, Tennessee. He married his sweetheart, Helen, and shortly after the wedding was transferred again, this time to Dalton, Georgia, the carpet capital of the world.

At that time he and Helen lived in Carbondale, a small town south of Dalton. They lived on Johns Mountain. Helen worked in Dalton, and every day at 4:30 P.M., Martin picked up his wife from work. Normally, they would drive up Johns Mountain almost to the top and turn left on Hilltop Road to their house. This day, however, Martin didn't turn left, but drove to the top of the mountain. He didn't know why he drove to the top; he had never been there before. At the top was an old cemetery, where he parked the car.

"What are we doing here?" asked Helen.

"I don't know," replied Martin, as he got out of the car. His wife joined him, and Martin, who to this very day doesn't know why, walked straight to an ancient gravestone. The name on the stone read Carter.

Martin, since he was twelve years old, was aware that he had a gift. He always seemed to know what was going to be said or what was going to happen within the next thirty minutes. It didn't work all the time, but if something bad were going to happen, Martin would sense it.

Martin and Helen left the cemetery and drove back down the mountain and home. At 5:30 P.M., the telephone rang for Martin. The message was: "Martin, your mother passed away at 4:45 this afternoon. I am sorry." Martin's mother's maiden name was Carter.

The Visionary

It's called a gift by some and a curse by others. It's the ability to see into the future. Some are born with it; others acquire it as they pass through life. Most never speak of it, but Heather did. She tells the story of her Aunt Maggie's experience. Margaret Boden was a spinster in her eighties. Her family had been one of the original settlers in the community. She was a small child when her father and uncle had built homes on the rich bottom-lands stretching between the low-lying mountains of Appalachia. They were farmers, living off the land, and this black earth promised a good life for the Boden family.

The children, all ten, grew up. Most married and moved away to the city, but Margaret, the youngest daughter, stayed. She never married, instead spending most of her adult life tending to the needs of her parents. When they died, she inherited the old home and stayed where she was. Content in the old ways, her needs were few and her wants little more. Selling part of the bottomland, Margaret was financially secure, and having lots of friends in the ever-growing town of Landers gave her even more reason to stay. She felt in her soul she wasn't made to live in the city.

Aunt Maggie had "the sight." Her grandmother had had it, and it had passed on to her. Even as a child, she could see things yet to be. Her brothers teased her, saying she was a witch, but her mother said she was blessed. Sometimes Margaret believed she was cursed because she often saw things too horrible to be true, yet true they were and did indeed come to be. One of the most painful visions Margaret had in her later years she couldn't speak of until it was well in the past. It preyed on her mind unmercifully, making her physically ill.

Finally, she spoke to her beloved niece about the vision. Heather was the favorite of her sibling's children; she had been named for her grandmother and had her sweet disposition. Heather, too, had the sight and treasured her aunt's confidence when she needed help trying to decipher dreams and visions or clarifying a "knowing." Heather, who'd married at sixteen, lived in the city with her family, but she realized "the sight" was not of the city, but born of blood with the old southern mountains and linked with love to the old woman she called Aunt Maggie. Heather's brother, Brian, had died, and Heather suspected Aunt Maggie's "taking to her bed" was a result of something she'd known about it, for the old woman had begun going downhill shortly before the boy became ill. Heather visited her aunt a week or so after the funeral, as Margaret was said to be too sick to attend.

"I saw it," said Aunt Maggie. "I saw it and knew I couldn't do anything about it. I've worried and prayed, but Heather, you know these things are but a warning to prepare us for what's yet to come."

"I know, Dear," said Heather, taking the small hand of her aunt as she sat on the bed beside the sick woman. "I know you're hurting. We all are, and you are not at fault," she continued tenderly.

The old woman shook her head sorrowfully. "But I was so scared, and I wanted to be wrong and I couldn't tell anybody, Heather. It just tore at my soul," the aunt sobbed.

They sat quiet for a bit, then Heather asked, "Can you tell me what you saw?"

85

"It will only hurt you," the woman answered.

"Yes, I'm sure it will, but I'm strong and I believe it will help you to get better," Heather said softly.

The old woman wept, then began. "I was washing dishes and looked up and saw Brian lying in a coffin. It scared me so bad I dropped a plate. It shattered, and I glanced down at the shards of glass on the floor and then back up. It was still there—that vision of Brian. He wasn't sick. I had seen him a few weeks earlier and had talked to him on the phone three days before. I know he wasn't sick. We talked about Christmas."

Heather handed her aunt more tissue. Aunt Maggie wiped her tearing eyes. "It will be okay, Dear," said Heather as she too wiped tears from her eyes. "No, he wasn't sick then. He became sick in February. They never knew what killed him until yesterday. We finally got the reports."

"What was it?" Aunt Maggie asked.

"Degos Syndrome. It's very rare, and doctors don't know much about it. He didn't have to suffer long though, and there was nothing anyone could do," Heather said. "So now you need to let it all go, all this guilt inside you."

"He looked nice in the walnut casket in that yellow shirt," Aunt Maggie said in a near whisper.

"Yes, Aunt Maggie. Brian did look nice in his yellow shirt resting in the walnut casket," Heather responded.

No one ever questioned Aunt Maggie's visions. They were always correct in life and in death.

The Dreamers

Dream Spirits have been associated with the southern Appalachian beliefs for generations. The Native Americans who once lived on these lands believed Dream Spirits gave them visions of their purpose in life. Dream Spirits also served as guardians, warning of dangers or evil. Dreamcatchers were often placed at the head of the bed or over the doorway of homes to catch evil dreams before they could enter the dream world. Even today many Appalachian foothill people stand strong, believing that dreams do indeed have a significant purpose in our lives. They pay heed to those warnings and rejoice in their promise of good fortune.

Many such beliefs concern water—if one dreams of rushing water, there is sure to be a raging fire. Another sign is the color of the water. If the water in the dream is muddy, trouble is evident. But crystal clear water in a dream is a sure sign of good things soon to come. The dream world is often considered the reverse of reality, giving cause for celebration or despair. A dream of death constitutes an addition to the family, either by birth or marriage. But death is expected when one dreams of a wedding or a new baby. Some Appalachian folk see dreams as windows into the future and have often seen their own lives follow step by step what was lived before in their dreams.

Some people are haunted by dreams reaching nightmare

proportion and are always searching for some kind of answer for the fear experienced when wrapped in the cocoon of sleep. Others merely see dreams as an escape from life's realities and long for the adventures they often find in sleep. Some dreamers don't remember their dreams at all. Some won't tell their dreams for three days, hoping they will come true. Others don't speak of their dreams before breakfast for fear their dreams will become a reality. Dreams can renew the weary, devastate the most assured, and sometimes allow us to review pieces of the past or maybe see into our tomorrows. Dreams ripple sleep, and only the dreamer can see through the darkness of the unconscious to touch the Dream Spirit within his own soul.

Stories and legends are born here in the Appalachian foothills, yet are often experienced by those not native to the area, some never having had any prior knowledge of these mountains or their lore. Perhaps they are sensitive to the spirits; maybe the timing is right, or maybe the foothill mountains just cry out to those who trod the same paths taken in times past. Valerie Hudson, a visitor from St. Simon's Island, was in north Georgia to visit Pam Carruth, proprietor of the Blue Ridge Books and Art Works Shop. The shop focused on regional books and crafts by local artists. The quaint little shop reflected past and present with all the charm of its location. Valerie was also there to enjoy the autumn season. She stood in the shop, just off the main street in Blue Ridge, Georgia, and admired some pottery. It was then she turned to a shelf containing books of ghost stories.

"I had a strange experience with some ghosts, I think," she said softly. "I don't know what else you would call them." Asked to tell her story, Valerie took a book from the table in front of her and admired its cover, then began. "It was autumn," she said, "about this time of year, when me and a friend of mine and our children were doing some camping through the area. That's when it happened." She replaced the book gently on the table and continued in a soft voice. "We stopped by a cousin's house for a short visit before going on to our campsite. She told us there was no need to drive for another hour to the designated place as there was a perfect location just off old Highway 5, between Ellijay and Blue Ridge. It had just been cleared for power lines. We decided we would check it out. We were, after all, tired and the children were restless.

"We found the place with no trouble, and it was the perfect camper's site. It was on a slight rise, with ample wood for our campfire and plenty of space to turn the children loose to do a bit of exploring on their own without going beyond sight of the camp itself. The night was warm and crystal clear as we made dinner. The air had the smell of autumn, and we were so pleased to have this place all to ourselves. Soon the night had us bathed in its hypnotic trance, and we slept. When morning was well past sun-up, we woke to an amazing view. The mountains were ablaze with color, and we savored our surroundings over coffee.

"'I had the strangest dream,' my friend said. "I dreamed there were people marching through our camp. Men, women, and children. They wore ancient clothes and just trekked right through where we are now.'

"'But we weren't here,' I stated.

"'No,' came the response. 'But how did you know?'

"'Because I had the same dream,' I answered. The campsite was later discovered to be near what was known as Whitepath. It was named after and home to a Cherokee who was chief during the removal of the Native Americans from this area. As the Trail of Tears began and his people left this site to join others on their march to the Oklahoma territory, it is said Chief Whitepath cursed those who would take his land."

Perhaps the campers, wrapped in hypnotic mountain sleep, caught a glimpse of those long-ago travelers who began their journey on the Trail of Tears. Perhaps the Dream

Spirit of the Cherokees was sent as a reminder of that long-ago march across the southern Appalachian foothills—the same earth where the campers sought solace and peace in their sleep.

*   *   *

Alice Newgen is a dreamer. Not the usual dreamer of nightmares, Alice has dreams in her dreams and finds they are directly on point or sometimes symbolic to either herself or someone close to her. On a warm September afternoon, Alice sat at a picnic table overlooking a pond with ducks swimming in it. The pond was in the north Georgia mountains of Gilmer County. As a child, Alice and her father, mother, and three-year-old brother lived in Black Mountain, North Carolina, where the dreams began.

The first dream of dreams came to her when she was eight years old. Alice's grandmother had passed away only three months before. It was late at night when her dream began. In her dream, she was, she explained, playing in the back yard of her home. It was not quite dark when suddenly a woman appeared before her, her grandmother, Grandma Beaver. Alice, although only a child, knew her grandmother had died. The woman spoke, saying, "I am here only for you, Alice."

Alice was not afraid; she was excited. She said to the woman, "I'll go get Daddy and Mama."

"No, Alice," the woman spoke softly. "They won't see me. I am only here for you."

In her excitement Alice ran into the house shouting, "Daddy, Mama, come quick. It's Grandma Beaver. She's out in the back yard."

"No, Alice," said her daddy. "It's not Grandma. She is gone, Sweetheart."

"But she's out in the yard," said Alice. "I'm talking to her."

More to appease the child than anything else, the

90

parents trouped out to the back yard with Alice. "See," her father said, looking around. "There's no one here."

"But there is," said the little girl; pointing a small finger in the direction of the apparition she claimed to see. "She's standing right over there."

Her mother smiled at her and said, "You can stay out here a little longer, but not too long. It's getting dark."

After Alice's parents left, Grandma Beaver said, "Alice, I am only here for you and I am going to take you someplace. Here, take my hand." In an instant, Alice and her grandmother were in the middle of what Alice described as a planet of some kind. It had a lovely garden with flowers and trees everywhere. Still holding her grandmother's hand, Alice was led down a path to a bubbling brook.

"Alice," said the woman, kneeling down to look the little girl in the eyes, "I want you to be aware of some things you may have to deal with later. Also, I want you to come here when it's your time. I am happy here, and you will be, too. You will have to make many difficult decisions when you are older, but know that I will be looking after you. You will have a gift. Come, Alice, give me your hand; it's time to go back now."

"Grandma, I want to stay with you. It's so nice here," said Alice, tearfully. She didn't want to lose her grandmother again.

"No, Alice. You can't stay here," the woman stated. As the old woman took the child's hand, Alice found herself immediately back in her room in her own bed. She woke up. It was so wonderful, she thought to herself. Alice never forgot that dream, one of many such experiences. Not only has the dream helped her when faced with difficult decisions, but it is one of her most treasured memories. It was only the first of many dreams that followed. Alice has a gift. She is a dreamer of dreams.

Twenty years passed, and Alice had married a fine young man from the west coast. Although she'd moved west with her husband, Steve, her heart was back in the mountains of north Georgia. Alice had completed her education and had two children, a girl and a boy. Still, all through the years, Alice had her prophetic dreams. She never told anyone, except her husband, about her premonitions. Her parents, William and Clarise, and Alice's brother, Glenn, moved to Chattanooga, Tennessee. Life moved on for all of them. Then, about eight years ago, Alice had another profound, prophetic dream, a horrible dream. Someone close to her would die. Alice felt sure it was her father who would be struck down. But when she received a telephone call from her mother, it wasn't her father who was gravely ill, it was her now twenty-four-year-old brother, Glenn.

Alice immediately flew to Chattanooga where Glenn was hospitalized. She stayed two weeks and Glenn seemed to be getting better, so she went back to her home and family in California. But the premonition of the dream still haunted her. Two weeks later, she received another telephone call; this one from Glenn's doctor. He sounded excited, yet somewhat fearful, as he said Glenn was to be moved to Atlanta, Georgia's Emory Hospital. The doctor said, "No one in Chattanooga has ever seen this disease Glenn has contracted. There are only seventy cases nationwide. Glenn has a disease called Degos Syndrome."

Alice immediately flew to Atlanta. In the two weeks she spent with her brother, they grew very close. She stayed in his room, and since she hadn't been around him all that much in eleven years, they had a lot of catching up to do. After two weeks, Alice was readying herself to go back home and Glenn, with a smile on his face, said to her, "Don't worry, Alice. I'll be seeing you again." On March 24 Glenn passed away and Alice came back for his funeral. It was so sad. The twenty-four-year-old was buried on Good Friday.

The next night, Saturday, Alice slept in Glenn's bedroom. She tossed and turned for a long while before falling asleep. About 3 A.M., something woke her. An apparition appeared, an oval frame with a strong golden hue. In the center stood her brother, Glenn. He smiled at Alice and said, "Everything is fine and you will be all right. You will make it through this ordeal." The apparition disappeared.

Alice, sober faced, said, "I never saw a vision like that before or since."

At the same time, Alice's mother, Clarise, had been dozing on the couch in the downstairs living room. Something woke her up, she said: "I really didn't see anything, but I felt a presence. Actually, I felt as if it were more than one presence. I heard a voice in my mind, and it was Glenn's voice. I sensed he was telling me that everything was going to be all right. I was not supposed to worry about him any more. He was happy. And all was calm."

Old Friend

When the Korean war started," said Edward Blake, "none of us fellows hanging around the Sugar Bowl ever heard of any-place called Korea. Now the Sugar Bowl was right on Main Street at the far end of the business district. The drugstore was on the corner, and the Sugar Bowl next door, then the Methodist Church. The Sugar Bowl was the high school hangout. We guys spent most of our free time there. Even after we graduated high school, we still met there. Rock, Jack, Charley, Harold, and I were the best of buddies, and we loved the good old soda fountain, the big overhead fans, the wire chairs, and the small glass tables.

"Anyway, we soon learned where Korea was, all of us, but Rocky was rejected. He had a punctured eardrum and was classified 4F. It's funny because Rocky was the sturdi-est of all of us guys. Rocky's dream was to be middle-weight boxing champion of the world. He was going to be in the amateur bouts in Atlanta. You know, not too many boxers come out of the north Georgia foothills," said Edward. "Well, I ended up in Korea in the 25th Infantry Division. I was there about six months when I had to take a wounded officer back to a MASH unit. Just as I was walking into the mess tent, I heard a shout.

"'Hey, Edward, what are you doing here?'

94

Old Friend

"'Harold,' I yelled, for there stood Harold Bane, grabbing me and yelling all the time. After we exchanged news of who, where, and when and if we were going home, Herbert got a solemn look on his face and handed me a letter he had received from home. In the letter was a newspaper clipping from our local newspaper. Well, it boiled down to Rocky Eugene Rocklan was killed in an automobile accident. I was devastated. I thought Rocky would be the only one of us who would have survived after this vicious war had ended. My folks didn't tell me about Rocky because of how close we were. Mama said later that she thought I had enough to worry about being where I was.

"Seven months later I was back in good old Pickens County. I got home on a Friday, and after spending Saturday and Sunday with all my kinfolk, aunts, uncles, and cousins, I needed a break. Monday afternoon I wandered down into town. Of course it wasn't there; where the Sugar Bowl had been now stood a pizza store. I went on in. A bunch of kids were hanging around, some I knew, most I didn't. None were my old gang or former schoolmates. So I went back home. After supper, I was feeling kind of antsy, so I told Mama I was going to take a walk. I ended up at the former site of the Sugar Bowl. The drugstore was still on the corner. So as I had done a thousand times before, I put my right foot against the storefronts where the pizza place met the drugstore. It was 6:05 p.m. Now back then in any town in southern Appalachia, come five o'clock, suppertime, folks said the streets were rolled up till seven. Nothing much moved in the towns then.

"I leaned against the storefront and noticed that rolling up the streets at suppertime was the only thing that hadn't changed since I went away. I let my mind drift; I guess I thought I was grown up. I supposed I'd get married and settle down. It was quiet on Main Street, no vehicle traffic, no pedestrians, no one but me. Maybe I'd go to college; the G.I. Bill would pay for my education, I thought.

"I turned toward uptown to look at the town clock. It read 6:23. Then I noticed someone walking down the street. He looked familiar, but I didn't recognize him. I turned away and thought about what I would do with the rest of my life. When I turned again and looked uptown, the fellow was only about forty or fifty feet away and my heart stopped. I straightened up and swore I couldn't be seeing what I was seeing. The man continued walking toward the corner, and as he passed me, not four feet away, he smiled at me. I stood mute. Stunned, I looked into his eyes. As he passed me, deep within my very soul I knew who it was. It was my pal, Rocky. To this day, I don't know why I didn't say anything, grab him, do something, but I couldn't move. I was paralyzed. When Rocky reached the corner, he turned to me, smiled, and went on around the corner.

"With all my strength, I tore around the corner and stopped. No one was there. The street was completely empty of all living things. I ran into the drugstore, but he wasn't there. I guess my buddy, Eugene Rocklan, took one last walk through town; maybe he knew I'd be there and had come to say goodbye to me. Well, that's my story," said Dr. Edward Blake.

Ghost in the Field

Alicia Chapman was about five years old when she and her family moved to the rural reaches of Murphy, North Carolina. The grandmother lived there, and her health was fast failing. Alicia's father was off to fight in the war, so the mother decided to move the family to the old homestead and care for the sick woman in her time of need. The home was old, yet comfortable, with overstuffed furniture in the living room fronting a large stone fireplace that took up one whole wall. The headboards of the two beds in the bedroom reached almost to the ceiling, and the footboards were nearly as high. They cradled soft, cloud-like featherbeds that were shaken and fluffed daily, then topped with bright-colored patchwork quilts. Trinkets and treasures were stuffed on corner shelves and in table drawers—probably, Alicia thought, long-forgotten presents given to her grandmother.

One day, Grandmother reached into a high bureau drawer and took out a rag doll with string hair, button eyes, and a sewn-on nose and mouth. She gave the doll to her granddaughter. Its dress was made from a flower sack, and its bloomers and socks were fashioned from faded cotton scraps. The doll had no shoes, and Alicia was always wrapping the doll's feet in pieces of her hair ribbons. Alicia loved the doll and spent hours during the long, cold winter days singing to her, rocking her, and having imaginary parties. The little girl named her Dolly.

Alicia's brother, Willy, was older and spent most of his time with a grown cousin named Ben, who took care of the animals and anything else that needed attention. Ben lived there, too, but he had his own little house built right onto the back of Grandmother's. It was just one big room, but Ben did his own cooking there on a black cook stove with its pipe running out and up the side of the house. He had a chair for reading, a slab-board table, two homemade cane-bottomed chairs in a corner, and a small cot-sized bed pushed against one wall. It was always dark at Ben's house, so Alicia didn't go there much even though Ben was a nice man and his eyes twinkled when he smiled. He whittled to pass the time. He helped Willy whittle a cow, like old Flossie, who lived in the barn. It didn't look much like a cow, but Willy was pleased.

Alicia remembers these things and the warnings to her and Willy from the older folks living there in the house. "If you go outside, don't go near that old house on the hill. It's haunted. People don't go there because it's dangerous. It's old and rotten inside, and nobody lives there; you could get lost, and nobody would ever find you," said Grandmother.

"Old man Buckhannon hung himself up there, and they never found his wife," said Ben one day when the little girl asked about the big house. "Just ghosts live up there now and they'll get you, so stay away from there." Both Alicia and Willy agreed never to go to the haunted house on the hill where a man hanged himself and his wife disappeared and ghosts lived and would get children.

Late spring brought warm weather and better health to Grandmother, and Alicia ventured outside to play when her mother hung out the wash to dry on Mondays. The field between Grandmother's house and the old haunted house was thick with jonquils, growing wild in bunches. Their yellow blooms danced and swayed in the midday breeze.

One Monday afternoon, when her mother went inside

to take care of yet another load of wash, Alicia decided that she would take Dolly and go pick some of the pretty yellow flowers. Hearing Willy and Ben hammering something in the barn, Alicia climbed through the old split-rail fence, pulling Dolly with her. She cautiously ventured up through the open field where the biggest patch of flowers grew. The haunted house loomed big and dark even in the sun, but Alicia wasn't going all the way to that house, not even real close, just to that patch of jonquils that was the tallest.

She could see everywhere, and it was okay. She could still hear the hammering from the barn. It wouldn't take long, the little girl reasoned, to pick a bouquet. Laying Dolly on the ground, Alicia began to pull the jonquils. She had four or five in her small hand when a shadow overtook her. Turning to look behind her, she saw something big, dark, and scary. It was clothed in rags, moaning painfully and reaching out to her. Alicia screamed and ran, fearing it was a ghost from the haunted house that was about to get her. She looked back once as she ran, and it still stood there, a rag-shrouded hulk with upraised arms. She continued to scream and run. Again she looked back and saw nothing, only a field dancing with jonquil blooms. Ben, Willy, and her mother all came running to see what was wrong.

"A ghost tried to get me," she cried. They all looked in the direction of the field where the old house stood. Only the house was there atop the hill. The field was empty. There was no ghost. Remembering Dolly, Alicia began to sob loudly. Ben and Willy searched the open field of wild jonquils, but it gave up nothing but a piece of hair ribbon that had once been tied around Dolly's foot to make a shoe.

The Welcoming

When the Carsons decided to move to the mountains, they were ecstatic. They thought moving from Atlanta's urban sprawl would be the best thing they ever did. Jerry and Elaine had looked all through the north Georgia mountains for their dream house. They did not find it. But they did find the ideal property; sixty acres with an old tumbled down house on it. They decided to build their dream house, and when the final papers were signed, they started clearing the land.

Ninety-year-old Native American Naomi Blackspur, a neighbor, told them the land was once Cherokee and suggested they check the bottomland for flint rock. This place, according to the Native Americans, was called a Pine Trace. The Carsons found bags of flint and many arrowheads. The soil was black, and this, according to Naomi, was the baking area. There was also a high mound of stones. This place, said Naomi, belonged to the earth and should not be disturbed.

Jerry Carson was bush-hogging the area where their new home was to be built while Elaine wandered around just looking and wool-gathering. As she strolled aimlessly through the Pine Trace, she looked down. There in her path lay a three-foot black snake.

The Welcoming

"I yelled," she said, "but Jerry couldn't hear me. Of course, I ran, but the snake wasn't interested enough to follow me. I walked to a pile of stones, and there was another black snake, a smaller one. It was as if it were waiting for me. I just kept walking." Elaine walked to the farthermost corner of the property, and there stood a trace of ancient trees. "I suddenly felt, well, sorrow. Then I heard many voices coming from the trace. I couldn't make out the words, or what was being chanted, but it sounded so sorrowful that I wanted to cry." It was coming on to noon, so she went back. Jerry, she knew, would be hungry. Together, they sat on a log and ate sandwiches; Elaine told him about the snakes and the chanting voices.

Jerry was watching something and seemingly not paying her words any attention. Suddenly he said, "Hey, there's a butterfly on your head." She brushed it off, but it came back and landed on her head again. Finally, as if some kind of game, it landed on Jerry's head then flew to Elaine's head. It began to fly back and forth between them. After about an hour, they decided to take pictures of the colorful, strange-acting butterfly.

The next day Elaine went to visit her neighbor Naomi. Naomi's house was unpainted and very small, yet very homey. Elaine told the old Cherokee woman about the snakes and the butterfly and the chanting voices sounding high in the trees. Naomi sat still for a while, then a twinkle appeared in her loving eyes and she explained, "I am glad. You see, according to our legends, the snakes and the butterfly are a symbol, a symbol of welcoming. You and your husband are wanted on this land. I am happy, too; I welcome you also."

Naomi sighed and continued, "I see from what you've told me about the voices that you too have the gift—the gift, as I have, of seeing and hearing things others are not aware of. You see, many years ago there was a terrible massacre on the land where we now stand at the trace of trees. Many

101

men, women, and children have heard the sorrowful chanting voices. I, too, have heard them in the past."

Jerry and Elaine Carson have lived in their mountain
dream house on this sacred Native American land many
years. And they have been very happy. They look forward
to the years ahead as the wind whispers through the tall
trees in the trace and the spirits of the Native Americans
chant their joys and their sorrows.

Beckoning Spirits

It was late, long into the early morning hours at a rural hospital in the north Georgia foothills. William Bennett was a patient there in the critical care unit. He had suffered a heart attack, and his condition continued to worsen daily, even with highly competent doctors and nurses tending to all his needs.

"It was a Wednesday," Nurse Connie Simms says, "when Mr. Bennett began to speak with someone unseen and unheard by others in the unit." A silence, a long breath, and then the nurse continues her story. "I hurried to the patient's bedside, believing he needed assistance of some kind."

"Yes, Mr. Bennett," Nurse Connie said. "Can I do something for you? Do you need anything?"

"No," the man responded in a far-away tone. "I'm talking to ghosts, two of them at the foot of my bed. Do you see them? Do you hear them?"

The nurse, seasoned in her profession, looked around the cubicle with its life-support equipment standing sentinel over the patient. "No, I'm sorry," she said, reaching to touch Mr. Bennett's fevered brow with a cool wet cloth. She continued to speak softly. "Do you know who they are?" Connie knew from her years of nursing experience that these things, these apparitions, really did appear to some in their time of critical illness.

"It's my cousin, Johnny, and my brother-in-law, Clayton," the patient answered. "They want me to go with them."

"Do you want to go?" Connie asked, continuing to wipe the sick man's forehead.

"I'm just too scared," he answered.

The nurse smiled and said, "If you want to go with them, I'll hold your hand if you think it will help." The old man returned her smile and nodded his head as tears slid from the corners of his eyes. Connie placed the wet cloth on a nearby table and took the old man's hand in hers. It was trembling and fever-hot, wrinkled with age and hard living, and like the rest of him, it was tired. William Bennett focused a glassy stare at the foot of his bed, whispered a few words, then closed his eyes slowly. In a matter of moments, the patient's pulse slowed and his breath became soft and shallow. Nurse Connie watched prayerfully as the monitors changed life-sign patterns. The heartbeat was all but a straight line, and respiration only slightly registered little wavy lines, where before jagged peaks and valleys had climbed and fallen across the monitor screen. *His time has come*, thought Connie, *and his family is here to take him away from the suffering, away from the machines and drugs that only keep him alive, but won't allow him to live.*

As breath was leaving and peacefulness began to settle over the sick room, Dr. George Radford, the man's physician, stepped into the unit cubicle. Seeing his patient's condition so near death on all the monitors, he called a code and began immediate resuscitating procedures. Within minutes, the monitors and machines were humming and beeping. The numbers were jumping, and lines dashed jaggedly up high and crashed low, only to climb again—the pattern Mr. Bennett had developed during the past few days.

None of the critical-care unit nurses spoke of what had happened, but they all knew they had witnessed something beyond anything medicine could offer those with no hope. The nurses went about their normal nursing duties, and doctors came and went as patients were checked and left in the station attendant nurse's hands. And William Bennett slept, calm and restful, seemingly suffering no ill effects from his ghostly visitation or his near-death experience. The next day, William didn't complain of much pain, and the doctor was pleased with his patient's bit of progress, even though the man's heart was still damaged and sick beyond repair.

When visiting hours came, Herbert Bennett was there to visit his brother, William. Nurse Connie saw Herbert as soon as he entered the critical-care unit. She quickly extended a welcome and updated the younger Mr. Bennett on his brother's present condition. After the medical status was conveyed, the nurse asked, "Is your brother a religious man?"

"No, not really," came the reply. "Why do you ask?"

Connie was a bit reluctant to speak of the experience, yet said, "He was talking with a cousin and his brother-in-law. He said they were ghosts."

The younger Mr. Bennett smiled and asked, "What time was this?"

"About midnight," came the answer.

"I was on my knees about then, praying, asking God to send William an angel. I guess He heard me and was answering a desperate plea for help in a time of trouble." There was no more need for words between the nurse and the patient's brother. Connie returned to the station desk, and Herbert went to visit his brother. Each knew the apparition seen by William Bennett had been angels. A few days later, in the late night, when the newness of morning was being born, William Bennett silently and peacefully died, leaving machines, monitors, and life-forcing drugs behind, to go with those who had come for him.

A critical-care unit nurse named Mark told this story, knowing spirits do indeed exist. "Maybe they're here because we need their help," said Mark. He smiled compassionately and continued, "Ghosts, spirits, angels. Whatever anyone wants to call them, they're all around us. Patients see them all the time."

Water's Edge

Sometimes cries through these old mountains aren't heard in life, but there are a few that even death can't stop. And the sounds grow more haunting in the memories of the mind. The man's eyes carry a far-away look as he scoots a little closer to the table and runs a hand through the gray whiskers of his beard. He has told the story before over the years, but neither the telling nor the passage of time has lessened the turmoil it creates in the memory of his yesterdays.

"It was a long time ago, I remember," he says in a gravelly voice. "I was just a young man—well, not really much more than a boy—when that girl come up missing. Don't recall her name, but folks come from all over to look for her. They probably covered ground in four or five counties. I know me and Josh Tatum went and helped with the search one Saturday. It was rainy and cold. Nobody found anything. It was like she'd just disappeared. We said we'd go help the next Saturday, but we didn't. Being young, I guess we found something we thought was better to do. Then time went by and she wasn't found, and finally the search for her was called off. All the talk of her died down and folks just seemed to forget about her.

"Me and Josh seen a picture of her. She was pretty, with

long brown hair and brown eyes. I guess she was maybe six-teen or seventeen. About the same age as us. Folks figured maybe she'd run off with a sweetheart, but her papa and mama said she didn't have one. It always bothered me how everybody just stopped looking for her." The man becomes quiet, as if reason is just beyond his grasp. He blinks and takes a deep breath. Sighing, he travels back through the decades to tell of a time that haunts him still.

"One day me and Josh was going fishing down to the creek. There was a real good deep fishing hole there where we always caught fish. We raced down a logging trail and climbed over some downed tree trunks and was just having a good time getting to the creek. When we reached the fish-ing hole, we noticed a big, black, plastic sack in the water. It was lodged against some old tree roots that were sticking up where the high water had washed the bank out. The hair on my neck prickled, and my stomach got shaky. I think Josh got spooked, too. We didn't go anywhere near that sack but decided we didn't want to fish that day and got away from there as quick as we could.

"Something made me call the sheriff about that sack, and I guess him or his deputy went to see about it, 'cause sure enough it was that missing girl. She was dead. Somebody had killed her and put her in that sack then threw it in the creek. Me and Josh went back there three times to fish, but every time we got to the water's edge, we heard the sound of somebody groaning, like they was hurting real bad. We never seen nobody. There wasn't even a sign of anybody there when we looked, but we could hear that groaning real and plain as anything. It was coming from where we saw that sack in the water. After the third time, we knew it must be sounds coming from that girl that was missing and killed. We never, either one of us, ever went back there again. That was a sound I didn't ever want to hear again, and I wonder if it's a sound I'll ever be able to forget."

The General

Henry and Marge Miller tell of a strange occurrence that happened to them. The Millers lived near the Chickamauga Battlefield in an old, but well-kept house. Built around 1857, the house was large. It wasn't a mansion, but sat on a good piece of ground. Marge relates the story as she recalls that night all those years ago.

"We were watching television, Henry and I, when there came a knock on the door. I went to see who it was. When I opened the door, I could see a horse and buggy parked in our driveway. A man stood on the porch. He asked me if someone I had never heard of was at home. I replied, 'There is no one with that name living here.' Now the man was young, not much older than a teenager, and he was very polite. He was dressed in old-fashioned clothing; since it was night, I couldn't quite make out exactly what he was wearing. But it looked like a Confederate uniform.

"When I returned to the sitting room, my husband asked, 'Who was it at the door?' I said, 'Some young man looking for someone. Must have had the wrong place.' I paused, then continued, 'He looked like he was wearing a Confederate uniform.'

"'Oh, that's possible,' said my husband. 'Probably in one of those Civil War reenactments. They are probably having one at the battlefield.' This was not surprising since many reenactments took place in our area all year long. I was always reading about them in the local paper. But I never expected one of the soldiers to appear at my door. My husband, Henry, is a real history buff. He has catalogued all the people who have lived in historical houses of the area since they were built. When I told him the name of the person that strange young man had asked for, Henry checked his notes and said there had never been anyone with that name living here in our house.

"One Saturday afternoon, Henry was at the local library to hear a historian speak on the Chickamauga battle and the people who lived in the area at that time. After the talk was over, Henry, remembering the young man, went up to the historian and asked if he knew the name and where that family had lived. The historian laughed and said, 'Yes, I know the name, and I think—no, I'm sure—he lived for a while in your house.' The man went on to explain how the name would not have been on any deed or registered in the courthouse.

"After Henry came home, he made a cup of coffee and thought about what he had learned from the historian. When I came home from shopping, he called me into his study. 'Marge,' he said, 'I found out a little about the man that young fellow was asking about last week.'

"'Oh, good,' I said, 'tell me about him.'

"'Well,' Henry said, sipping his coffee, 'It's a strange story. You see, there was no reenactment of a battle last week.'

"'Who, then, was the young man dressed as a southern soldier knocking at our door?' I asked.

"'I don't know,' Henry answered. 'We will probably never know who he was. But that person he asked for did live here for a short time. You see, Marge, this house, our house, was the temporary quarters of General Braxton Bragg of the Confederate Army. The young soldier was probably asking to see his commanding officer, the General.'"

Spirits on the Autumn Wind

It was late autumn in southern Appalachia, a time when the kaleidoscopic colored leaves rustle in the wind, when days are still warm and the chill in the night bites in warnings of winter just around the corner. It is a time when all is still and you can hear the quiet and almost hear what it is saying. Autumn is nature preparing for the best and worst of a season yet to come. Some old folks believe and say that spring and fall are times for the aged and sick to die, that nature knows they can't make it through the coming season. Death is marked for many by the rising and falling of the tree sap.

It is not known whether Nelly Coulver held these beliefs true or not, but her son, Richard, believes she knew when it was her time to die. Richard looked after his mother for the last twenty-five years of her life. She was a good mother and a good person. Together, they built a house in the mountain foothills, and the old woman did indeed enjoy her life and the splendor of her family and surroundings. Richard had a job as a security guard for a mountain community and resort. Even though it was night shift, it was a job he enjoyed, especially on those crisp, chilly nights when a jacket felt good and the coffee in his thermos warmed him all the way down.

One such night was filled with not only the job but also a touch of mystery and the true reach of his mother's love. It had been rather busy; people with time-shares had come from all over to spend the last warm days in the Georgia mountains. The foliage was beautiful, and apple orchards offered their bountiful harvests. The small mountain town always drew a crowd during this time of year, for the apple festival and fall color tour had been advertised for weeks. All the resort condos, cabins, and campsites were filled. It was nearing daylight, Richard remembers, that time just before day is born. The sky was ribboned in varying shades of pinks and golds in the far-away east, and stars still twinkled against a deep navy over the rest of the heavens.

Richard just sat for a bit admiring the beauty of the heavens and drinking the last of his coffee. He watched as the day birthed in the quiet of the mountain morning. It was then that Richard heard someone call his name, whisper quiet, almost beyond the reach of sound. He looked around only to find himself alone in the beginning dawn. It happened two more times, but there was no one anywhere. Once Richard felt a hand caress his face but decided it must have been a mere breeze. He was, after all, very tired. But the feeling of a presence—unknown and unseen—and the faint sounds of his name being spoken gave him cause for unease. What was it? Who was it just beyond the reach of his senses?

Richard was relieved when his shift was over; he drove home in silence, enjoying the stillness. The feelings of an unseen presence, the near whispering sounds, and the almost touch had disappeared, had gone; nothing unusual prickled his senses. He was just tired and weary from the long night's work, he thought; with a few hours sleep, any anxiety would resolve itself. Returning home, Richard found his mother dead. She had died in her sleep. The estimated time of her death, according to the attending physician, was

6 A.M., the exact time Richard had felt an unseen presence and heard his name whispered on the light autumn wind.

"She came in spirit to tell me all was well with her and to say goodbye," said Richard in a soft, deep tone. Then taking a long slow breath, he continued, "She had a good soul, a kind spirit, and I'm sure I'll always miss her. But I'll always cherish her last act of love toward me, her farewell in the early dawn of autumn, just as the day was being born."

The Depot

Back in the good old days in southern Appalachia, no matter how small a town was, the trains stopped there. Sometimes the passenger trains came only once or twice a day. Freight trains, though, plied all through the day and night, bringing all sorts of merchandise while hauling away logs, marble, and other raw materials from the mountains to the cities to meet the public's demand. In a small town in East Tennessee, the depot would close at 6 P.M. An hour later, the younger folk would pile in old jalopies and head for the depot's parking lot. Some would spoon, while others drank beer, home brew, or any other alcoholic 'shine they could get.

One night two young men drank a lot more apple brandy than was good for anybody, boy or man. It was late in the night when most of the teenagers left and went home. Still later that night, the sheriff was called because the loitering was still going on. When he arrived, he found the young men in their car, dead, the automobile crushed like a tin can. According to the railroad report, when the Express roared through the town and passed the depot, the engineer saw a car on the tracks. Unable to stop the train, he smashed into the vehicle. After checking with the young folks around town, it was determined that the two

114

victims found in the car were in a drunken stupor when they parked on the tracks.

The glory days of the railroad are over. The trains no longer stop at the small, rural, outreaching depots. The railroad tracks are overgrown with weeds, and a train hasn't run there in over thirty years.

Billy Stevenson tells of another tragedy that happened at the old depot. After the trains stopped and the depot boarded up, a new generation used the parking lot. Kids and young guys and gals used the parking lot as those other youths had years before. "We'd go there with our sweeties," said Billy, "and neck. Others went there to drink, and many drank themselves stupid. On the night of one strange and sinister event, I was there with my high school sweetheart. About eight or ten cars were parked in the old depot parking lot. The lot was pockmarked with potholes, and most maneuvered their vehicles around them carefully. It was a warm spring night with a full moon. My girlfriend and I were talking about our graduation coming up in only three weeks. She talked about going on to college. I really wasn't sure about college because I didn't have the money. I said I might go into the Army instead.

"'Hey, look,' my girl said. 'Those two boys are driving up to the old tracks.'

"'Boy,' I said, 'some guys can really be stupid. They'll probably get a flat tire.'

"'Well, at least they won't get hit by a train,' she said. About fifteen minutes later, we left the old depot. Her parents were really strict about whom she went out with and when she should be home. I didn't want to get her into trouble. I really liked this girl.

"The next day at school everyone was talking about what had happened the night before. When I heard about the tragedy, I hurried to find my buddy, Joe Cox. He had been parked next to us at the train depot. 'Joe,' I asked, 'what happened after we left last night?'

"'Billy,' he said, 'it was the craziest thing. Those two guys who were driving around the depot in that old car finally drove off and parked right on the tracks.' In a strained voice, Joe continued, 'A couple of us got out of our cars and yelled at them to get off the tracks. But they just cussed at us. Oh, they were crazy drunk and no one could talk to them. We were just getting back in our cars when someone yelled, 'Look!' And we could see a light coming down the tracks. Well, to tell the truth, we all tore out of there. I tell you, Billy, that light looked like a train light coming down the tracks,' Joe stammered. He was trembling and perspiration beaded his brow. He took a long, deep breath and continued, 'Around midnight, a police car went to the depot parking lot to check things out. They found a crushed car with two young guys in it, dead. It couldn't have been a train, I don't think, but we all saw the light, and it all happened at the exact same spot those other two men got crushed to death by a train all those years ago.'"

Going Home

Elder family members living with their children are common here in the mountain foothills of Appalachia. Family is the core of one's being and cherished more highly than any monetary treasure.

This was the belief of Ann's family. Ann is a nurse, a caregiver in one of the small hospitals dotted about the low-lying north Georgia mountains. She tells of her grandmother who lived with her children and their families for more than forty years. Grandmother decided she wanted to go home—her home—to live. The children and grandchildren all got together and decided if it was Grandmother's true heart's desire, they would indeed move the old woman back to the home of her younger years. After all, being a large family, there were certainly enough of them; they could take turns staying with her.

The old home place had been kept in the family over the decades and modernized somewhat as time had passed and money had afforded. Soon after Grandmother's return to her beloved home, she fell and broke her hip. Her health began to slide away. It wasn't long until her kidney functions slowed and her appetite was all but gone. The family gathered, worried and concerned their beloved grandmother would not survive this ordeal. One visitation to the sick-room, just to peek in, found the old woman crying, broken-hearted. When asked what was wrong, Grandmother answered in a weak voice that they wouldn't let her come. She was deeply upset and continued to cry and repeat herself. A family member tried to soothe the sick woman, holding her hand gently and asking, "Who? Who won't let you come, Dear?"

Grandmother answered, "Ben. My Ben won't let me come. And Mrs. Galloway. Ben and Mrs. Galloway said I couldn't come yet." Ben, her husband, had been dead some forty years. And Mrs. Galloway, a friendly neighbor woman who had lived up the road, had died about ten years earlier. So it was they who had told Grandmother she couldn't come yet. She had to wait. Soon after the disturbing visitation from her beloved husband, Ben, and her dear friend and neighbor, Mrs. Galloway, Grandmother's physical health began to improve.

Almost a year has passed and so have most of Grandmother's memories, as Alzheimer's has claimed yet another mind once filled with yesterday's thoughts of love, family, life, and wonderment. "Grandmother doesn't recognize any of her family any more as this disease has advanced quickly," says Ann, "Yet she speaks often of her dear husband, Ben, my grandfather, and of her friend, Mrs. Galloway, saying she is sure they are waiting for her and she must soon get ready to go."

The Plantation

The Kings, Ralph and Lydia, looked forward every year to their summer vacation. The last week in July and the first week in August was their usual break from high-tension jobs. This year, while Lydia got the usual two weeks, Ralph got to take only one week because of job pressures.

"Well," said Lydia, "what are we going to do for just one week? I don't mind lolling around the second week, but we should do something special together when you are off work."

"I don't know," said Ralph, "but we'll think of something."

So the vacation plans were put on hold until the first of June. Then Lydia received a telephone call from her sister, Flora, in Virginia inviting the Kings to spend a week with them. Lydia told Flora that they would be up to their place in southwestern Virginia the third weekend in July.

"Great," said Ralph, "we should have a good time with Flora and Jack." Jack was Flora's husband.

"Another thing, Flora's son, Dan, will be home from college and Flora said he would be glad to be our guide."

Finally, it was vacation time, and the Kings loaded up their car for the three-hundred-mile trip to Virginia. They left early on a Saturday morning, stayed overnight in a motel, and arrived at their destination early the next Sunday morning. While Flora and Lydia caught up on family news, Jack and Ralph played golf. Early in the week, Dan, Lydia's nephew, squired his aunt and uncle around the local historical points of interest. Ralph, an avid amateur photo bug, took many snapshots with his new camera, a birthday present from his wife.

On Wednesday morning, Dan said, "I have a treat for you today. We are going to visit an old plantation. It belonged to a Colonel Morgan. I doubt if anyone in the family is still living there; the last descendant was an old woman who must have been about ninety, and that was some time back." Although it was warm when they left, there was a cool breeze, and the Kings enjoyed the ride through the back roads of rural Virginia. They left the highway and drove down a dirt road. There was no traffic at all. Dan turned the car into a long rutted driveway. Everywhere weeds had grown tall, and it looked as if they were the first to drive up the driveway in years. Then the driveway ended in front of an antebellum mansion of large proportions.

"Wow," smiled Ralph, "this place is beautiful. You sure no one lives here?"

Puzzled, Dan said, "I don't think so. The family is all gone as far as I know."

The main house of the plantation property looked to be in very good shape. Some paint had peeled and the grounds looked untended, but all in all, the Kings marveled at the once beautiful home.

"Can I help you?" asked a feeble voice. They turned, and there stood an old woman—an ancient woman—with a twinkle in her eyes.

"Oh," said Lydia, "We're sorry we bothered you. We're from north Georgia, and my nephew is showing us the wonderful area here in southwest Virginia."

The Plantation

"Would you like to come in and see the place?" asked the elderly woman.

"Oh, yes," answered Ralph and Lydia together. As stated, the woman was old, how old none of the three could guess, but she led them into the mansion, and upon entering the front door, all were awestruck. Wonderful paintings hung on the wall; one, she informed them, was her great-grandfather, Colonel Morgan. The furniture was old, but in good shape. The rooms were large and airy; all in all, as Lydia said later, "It was the best old mansion tour Ralph and I have ever been on." Finally, they had to leave and said goodbye to the smiling, ancient woman. She didn't know why, but Lydia hugged her and wished her well. Ralph, who had been taking pictures of the plantation, asked, "May we take a picture of you sitting on the couch with my wife and me?"

"Why, of course," she giggled. The three sat on the couch, Ralph on the left, the old lady in the center, and Lydia on the right. Lydia held the woman's hand as Dan took several pictures. Goodbyes were said again, and the Kings and Dan drove away. Lydia was quiet as Dan and Ralph discussed the plantation and their gracious hostess.

"There is something wrong about today," said Lydia. But she could not say what it was. The Kings, after their week's stay in Virginia, said their goodbyes to their hosts and drove back to Georgia. Ralph went back to work, while Lydia relaxed at home on her second week off.

On August 10, 1991, Ralph picked up the developed film of the pictures he'd taken at the plantation. He rushed into the house and shouted, "Lydia, I have the pictures of our vacation." They laughed as they pored over Ralph's fine photography of their vacation.

"Hey," he said, "here are the snapshots of the plantation."

"Let me see them," said Lydia. Taking the photographs from her husband, she looked through them carefully. "I told you something was wrong about that place. And this

121

proves it," she said in a trembling voice. She handed Ralph four of the pictures Dan had taken.

"Why, the old woman isn't in any of them," said a stunned Ralph. "There I am, and there you are, but in the center where the old woman sat is just empty. And in all four pictures Dan took, it's the same."

"What I meant when I said something was wrong," began Lydia, "was when I hugged the old woman, she felt cold. And when we sat for the picture taking and I held her hand, it, too, was ice cold like you would expect somebody dead to be."

The Haunted Cupboard

Way back in the late 1890s, folks were more charitable than they are nowadays. When strangers roamed through the southern Appalachian mountains, they could always be sure to find a meal. Many folks traveling through the area, when out of food, could knock on the door of any cabin and get something to eat. Sometimes the people who lived in these isolated areas didn't have much, but what they had, they shared.

There were certain men who did not have homes for whatever reason; maybe they had lost their property to taxes, or maybe nature had played havoc with their crops. There were probably a number of reasons such men were homeless. Some said this harkened back to their Scottish heritage, living from one odd job to another. Old men wandering through the Highlands, doing chores, could always get a place to stay for a few days and some food. These men usually had a route they followed, coming to the same homes about the same time every year.

Bud Taylor was one of this type. He roamed the mountains of the Appalachian foothills, usually stopping at the same places each year. Now, old Bud wasn't a moocher. He would work for his keep; whatever folks asked him to do, he would gladly do it for a couple of days of free room and board. Ernest Evans tells the story that Bud told until his death in 1909. When Bud stopped at the Evans' place, he was immediately put to work. He chopped firewood, did some carpentry, or whatever else the Evans family asked him to do. One night, Bud was sleeping in a small pantry off from the kitchen. It was long after midnight when he woke up hungry. Mrs. Evans had told Bud that if he got hungry during the night, just to help himself to anything in the kitchen cupboard.

The Evans' grandfather had passed away three days before Bud's visit to the Evans household, and the cupboard was filled with vittles the neighbors had brought for the man's funeral and day-before visitors. Bud Taylor walked out to the kitchen and headed for the cupboard. He said later, "I sure was hungry." He opened the cupboard door, screamed, and slammed it shut.

"I couldn't believe my eyes," he told. Bud then slowly opened the cupboard door again and the same scene appeared before him. "There it was, a living image of Grandpa Evans." Again he shut the door, more softly this time. He then yanked it open, and to his shock, there again stood an image of Grandpa Evans. Feeling a bit more sure that he really was seeing the grandfather, Bud said, "Mr. Evans, Sir, I thought you was dead." Bud Taylor swore for the rest of his life what happened next was absolutely true. "The old man just seemed to stand there staring at me, and I could've swore for spit that I heard him say, 'Well, I guess I am.' And then that old man, well, he just vanished."

Bud, no spring chicken himself at the time of this happening, has since passed on to the next life, but he always told the story of Grandpa Evans in the pantry, three days after his death, for truth, sure as bears live in the woods!

Civil War Ghosts

The Civil War was fought all over these foothill mountains. Many skirmishes were fought, won and lost, and never recorded in the history books. Many battles left no survivors to tell the agonizing tales. Yet some cry out to be remembered on the light summer winds of time. And sometimes they are heard.

Joanne Goeckel was born in the Yankee north and in 1957 moved to the foothill mountains of Georgia with her parents to live on a farm at Sugar Creek. She was a shy ten-year-old, mostly arms and legs, but she could ride a horse like a professional. Lightning, her horse, a fleabag gray, knew her commands simply by her body's movements and responded accordingly. One evening, Joanne went out to feed her horse. It was steel cold wintertime, and an icy breeze danced through the trees and teased her long brown hair. With a bucket of feed in her hand, she persuaded Lightning to come near the pasture fence. She always shared the day's secrets and events with the big animal during feeding time, even on nights as cold as this.

As she reached the pasture fence, the breeze quickened and the air grew bone-hurting cold and heavy. The low mumbling voices of many men hung in the air. Lightning, his eyes wild and rolling, jerked his head back,

125

tore the reins from Joanne, bolted, and ran. Joanne, still hearing the voices, looked about quickly. She didn't see anybody in the night. There was nothing visible but a million stars sprinkled on a velvety sky. The voices were coming nearer, and added to them were the clanking of trace chains and the creak of wagon wheels rolling over uneven earth. There were horses or mules snorting and whinnying, along with the clomping of heavy hoofs. The girl was afraid. Her heart pounded like roaring thunder. The noise surrounded her, yet she saw nothing. At the sound of many marching feet, she threw the feed bucket and ran. She ran from something that mashed heavy on her, threatening to suck the air from her lungs.

It was later told to Joanne by Annie Russell, an old woman nearly one hundred years old, that back in 1864, during the Civil War, General Hood's Confederate troops had been separated from the main southern front. And after three weeks of wretched rain, part of them had camped on the creek where the fence stood. Before the troops broke camp and began the march to rejoin General Joe Johnston's division, enemy soldiers surprised them and a skirmish broke out. No record was ever made of this outbreak, nor of how many soldiers were injured or maybe killed. Years later, Civil War artifacts were found when the pastureland was terraced to prevent erosion. Noted historians were informed of the find and did investigate the site to confirm the story told decades ago by Annie Russell.

Joanne never questioned the old woman's story, knowing she herself had somehow heard it on the wind as it blew back through time almost a century.

The Fisherman

Jack Kelley pulled into the driveway of his three-year-old home in Pickens County, Georgia. He was faced with a major decision. Should he, or shouldn't he, quit his job? As he entered the large well-built house, his wife, Elaine, met him at the door. "Tough day at the office, Honey?" she asked.

"Yes," he answered, "and it's getting tougher every day."

"Just rest a minute, Dear," said the worried Elaine. "Dinner isn't quite ready yet." She could see the stress on his face.

Jack sat down on the sofa and thought, oh boy, the monthly mortgage on this place would have bought my grandfather's farm. But I don't think I can take much more. I have to quit that job; it's just too much for me. After dinner as the Kelleys sat on their deck in the warm spring evening, Elaine said, "Jack, whatever you do about your job, I'll be with you." Jack looked across the valley at the view of the north Georgia mountains he loved so much.

"Thanks, Honey, it's just I get so stressed out. I don't seem to have any time for relaxation."

"Jack," smiled Elaine, "I remember when we were going to high school, and if I'm correct, didn't you used to play hooky every so often and go fishing? Why don't you go tomorrow? It's Saturday, and you won't be playing hooky."

Jack laughed, "You know, Elaine, I haven't been fishing for years. Maybe that's a good idea. And I still have my old fishing gear in the garage."

The next morning Jack was down by the river. It was a warm spring day, and luckily no one else was fishing at Jack's favorite old fishing spot. He dozed, fished, and thought nothing but good thoughts, especially thoughts of his sweet wife, Elaine. He had about decided to quit his high-stress, high-paying job. But they'd have to let their house go, and he worried how they would live. Besides, Elaine loved their home. And what if he couldn't get another job? Jack looked up; about eight feet away sat another man. Gosh, he thought, I didn't even hear him arrive. The man was middle-aged and looked sad. Jack had seen him around before but didn't know him. Suddenly, the man hooked a fish and pulled it in. Over the next hour, the man caught four more fish while Jack had yet to get a bite. Finally, Jack yelled at his fellow fisherman, "What are you using for bait?"

The man replied, "Just worms, want to try some? And why don't you try your luck over here?"

"Yes," said Jack. "Oh, my name is Jack Kelley. I live here in the new development, but I was born and raised here in Pickens County."

"My name is William Graham," said the man. He looked at Jack, crinkled his brow, then said, "Say, you look a little down or, well, depressed. Care to talk about it?"

"Yes, I guess I am a little down. I'm deciding about my job—should I quit it or not. I don't feel I can handle it any more. So I guess I'll just quit it, although I'll never get another job like it."

William nodded, then concentrated on fishing. Finally he said, "You know, Jack, I quit and it was the stupidest thing I ever did." William said with a sad look on his long face, "I got to the point where I felt I was going nowhere fast, too. I thought I was at the end of the line. So I just quit. It was a shock to my family, and it really hurt them badly.

The Fisherman

If I were you, Jack, I'd reconsider quitting your job. It's not what it's cracked up to be." William caught three more fish. Jack caught only one fish all day, but he didn't care. Talking to William made him realize he was maybe, just maybe, not thinking as a responsible adult.

"Well, Jack," said William as the sun began to go down, "I have to be off. I'm going on a trip. So good luck, and think hard about quitting." Then he left. Jack fished a little while longer. He was a bit more relaxed. He leaned back against a tree, yawned, and thought, well, it's been a good day, but it's getting late, so I guess it's time to pack it in.

On the way home, Jack stopped at the local convenience store to get gas. He went into the store to pay for the gas and noticed some former schoolmates. They were just hanging around as they often did when back in school.

"Hey Jack," yelled Buddy Norton, "You catch any fish?"

"Just one," smiled Jack.

"Nobody seems to be catching any fish," said the store-owner, Ed Sanders.

"Yes," said Ron Engle, "I went this morning and not even a bite."

"Oh, I don't know," said Jack. "A fellow fishing alongside me caught over a half a dozen."

"Who was that?" asked Buddy.

"A guy named William Graham," was Jack's reply. There was complete silence in the store, not a sound.

Then Ed Sanders said, "You didn't see William Graham. He died last Tuesday. He was buried yesterday."

"Yeah," cut in Ron Engle, "he committed suicide last Tuesday. He just up and quit it all."

The Search

William Crowe was twenty-nine years old when he was found inside his car in the garage-workshop, dead. An autopsy showed carbon monoxide poisoning. His death has always been a puzzle to his family and friends, who believed they knew the man so well. William had a good-paying job and was considered a solid employee, at the same company for eleven years. A religious man, he was, and he and his wife, Jane, had two children. Their marriage was a happy one, according to Jane, with no more problems, and maybe less, than average. They had a mortgage, a car payment, and utility bills. But that was all the money they ever spent except for general household spending. They had even managed to save a few dollars over the years, so there didn't appear to be any money problems. There were no answers to the man's death, and it was never known whether he committed suicide, died accidentally, or was murdered.

But the health of William's father, Herman, suffered as a result of losing his son, and several weeks later, he moved into his son's home to be cared for by Jane. There was no other family, and his daughter-in-law couldn't bear the thought of her children losing their beloved grandfather so soon after their father. The nearest nursing home was some fifty miles away.

The Search

One evening, Herman saw his son go into the garage. Herman even recognized the clothes he wore. The old man hurried outside to the garage but found no one there. Over and over this happened, and each time the father hurried to the garage, hoping to find his son, but could never get there in time. William always disappeared before the old man arrived. One evening, a neighbor lady, while driving by, saw a man going into the Crowes' garage. She backed her car up and stopped. She then got out and hurried to the front door. When Herman opened the door in answer to the frantic knocking, the lady was trembling.

"You'd better hurry," she said. "I just saw a man going into your garage."

Herman shook his head sadly and with tearing eyes replied, "That's all right. It's just William. He's looking for something. I just wish I knew what he's looking for. If I knew, I would take it to him."

Warlock's Home?

When Bobby Kendall was a teenager, back in the 1970s, getting a new automobile was the ultimate joy. On his seventeenth birthday, his folks bought him a new car. So Bobby and the guys rode around East Tennessee looking for girls and any other fun they could find.

One night, Eddy Merrian said, "Let's go out to the Warlock's Place." The Warlock's Place was way out in a rural area of east Tennessee. The story goes that back in the 1920s, a warlock lived in a fine manor. No one today can recall where the story came from that the man was a warlock. Whoever he was, he lived alone, and no one, it was said, ever visited him. The legend says that he got in an argument with a local merchant about some rotten feed, and the so-called warlock put a curse on the merchant. From then on, the merchant suffered every tragedy known to man and finally one night he hanged himself.

One dark night in 1925, a group of men from the merchant's hometown set out to destroy the warlock. What happened that night is lost in time. What is known is they tried to burn the warlock's home down. The fire raged all through the night, but when daybreak arrived, the house still stood with only minor damage. The local sheriff investigated, but no arrests were made and no one ever saw the supposed warlock again. "We found no trace of the man or any signs of bloodshed," reported the sheriff. Time passed, and most folks forgot about the warlock. But his house still stood, and occasionally adventurous teenagers would go there. It was funny, some folks said, that the kids never spoke of what happened out there. The house had changed over the years. It now sported a bright green roof. No one knew what this meant, if anything.

So Bobby Kendall and his buddies went joy riding that night and ended up at the Warlock's Place.

"Better leave the motor running, Bobby," said Hank Sickles.

"Yes," agreed Johnny Bowers. "You never know when we might have to bug out in a hurry."

Three of the teenagers walked around outside the old house while Bobby went inside. He walked through the rooms on the first floor. Most of the walls were bashed in, and trash littered the floors. Bobby entered a room on the first floor. It looked like it might have been a bedroom. The moon had risen; looking out through a busted out window, he could see two of his friends milling around in the yard. "To tell the truth," Bobby said later, "I felt kind of funny. I guess when I walked in that room, I was a little scared. But I could still hear the car motor running, so I just sighed and laughed at myself." Bobby had just turned away from the window when he heard a gasp. Looking back, he saw Eddy Merriam and Johnny Bowers, both white as ghosts.

Bobby went back to the window and asked, "What's the matter with you guys?"

Eddy was waving his arms but couldn't speak. Johnny, looking faint, shouted, "Look out Bobby! There's somebody behind you and he's reaching out to grab you!" Bobby spun around and, seeing no one, ran through the hallway just wanting to get out of the Warlock's Place. He could hear the car horn blowing, and when he hit the porch running for all he was worth, he could see the car's lights were on as well.

The automobile horn was echoing through the valley, and Bobby thought one of his friends was warning him. But when he got to his car, there was no one in it. He couldn't stop the horn from bellowing. His three friends came running, and they all jumped into the car.

"Let's get out of here!" shouted Hank.

The car, despite the motor running, would not move. Finally the lights blinked once, then twice, and went out. The horn stopped blaring, and as soon as Bobby stomped on the accelerator, they sped away.

"I'm telling you, Bobby," said Johnny, "whatever that was at that house was just about to grab you."

"Yes," said Eddy, "I thought it had you. I was never so scared in my life."

"What was it?" asked Bobby. "And who turned the car lights on and started honking the horn?"

"I don't know what it was," answered Johnny. "But he had a cape on and long claw-like fingers. And if I can live to get out of here, I'll never come back here again."

All three boys denied they put on the lights or honked the horn. They were all on the side of the house when everything started happening. So today it sits as it has for seventy years with its green roof and its own secrets, known simply as the Warlock's Place.

The Wood Cutters

Three generations of Davis men were clearing a portion of their newly purchased land and cutting the pulpwood. The land was to be used as a field to grow corn come spring, and early winter was always considered the best time to cut timber. The sap was generally down, making the long tree trunks easier to manage. The men had worked hard all day, and before they realized it, dark was upon them. They lacked only one ridgeline being through felling the trees. An old shack on the other side of a rusted barbed-wire fence marked the boundary line for the land, and the men decided to stay the night there rather than go home and have to return in the morning for only a couple of hours. Besides, the oldest Davis man reminded the others that the headlights on the old truck hadn't worked in years.

The youngest man, Brad, wondered if the old shack was maybe once a hunter's cabin as there was a pot-bellied stove, a couple of chairs, and an old iron bedstead inside. He asked his grandfather. The old man wasn't sure, but agreed it was a good possibility as this land was considered prime hunting land. The men dragged the old stove close to the broken window and managed to shove the old fallen-down stove pipe with its rusty elbow joints together and stick it through the broken window and attach the other

135

end to the stove. Plenty of wood lay around, and since they hadn't eaten all the fried chicken and cornbread sent by the elder Mrs. Davis, they would be set till morning when they could finish the job and then head home.

After going to sleep, the three men were suddenly awakened by a scream, followed by a baby crying. Before they could discover the origin of the sounds rending the night, the threesome heard gunshots. They quickly grabbed their boots and coats and ran for the old truck where they spent the remainder of the night. As dawn broke and there was enough light to see, the noise of the old truck's engine cranking echoed through the stillness. Cold and scared, the grandson drove the old truck down the mountain. After they forded the creek, a small house came into sight around a bend in the road. A woman was seen standing on the porch. Brad stopped the truck, and the three got out and went and asked the woman about the shack they had stayed in and the screaming and crying. They asked if someone could have been shooting up there in the middle of the night.

The woman looked at the three men as if they were somewhat foolish to even go about the old shack. She informed them that many years ago, the man living there had gone crazy, killed his wife and child, and thrown their bodies down the well before he shot and killed himself.

Ellen's Brother

Mary Morgan and Ellen Dunn were average teenagers in the late 1960s. They played all the records of pop artists of the time. They had gone to school together since the first day they attended the small mountain school in the mountains of north Georgia. On a day they thought was just a regular day, an eerie event happened that to this day they cannot explain. Mary tells what happened that warm, late autumn day in 1969.

"After school, Ellen Dunn and I went to the county library. We were just fooling around and not in any hurry to go home. Finally, the library was closing and it was just before dusk when we started walking home. We giggled and laughed as we talked about our lives and what was going on at school—who was going with whom, and who broke up with whomever. We walked past where the old primary school had stood. It's gone; there's an office building there now. We just walked past the cemetery, and it was only a short walk until I was home: just across the bridge over the river and turn right onto the dirt lane that leads to our home. Ellen lived about a half-mile farther down past the bridge. We had just turned on the old dirt road leading to the bridge when I saw someone standing on the bridge. He was just standing there, looking down at the river. He looked young, although a little older than Ellen or me. Suddenly I stopped and said, 'Ellen, that looks like your brother, Bob.'

"'Yes,' she answered. 'It sure does look like Bob. But it couldn't be him; he's in Vietnam, and he's not due back for six more months yet.'

"The closer we got to the bridge, the more the young man looked like Bob Dunn. As we approached the bridge, he suddenly turned and looked at us, smiled, and in a flash he disappeared. After leaving Ellen on the other side of the bridge, I hurried up the lane and home. I told my mother and Aunt Adele what we had seen. Both my mother and aunt shook their heads knowingly. Mother said, 'We'll call the Dunn family after supper. But this could mean bad news.' I went to my room, for I too knew what seeing Bob Dunn on the bridge could mean. Ellen and I had maybe seen a ghost, a ghost of Ellen's brother, Bob. I was sure it meant he had been killed in action. My mother and my aunt both felt the same way. I heard them talking about what we had seen. When Daddy came home and was told what we had seen, he nodded as if to agree with Mama and Aunt Adele. After supper Mama called the Dunns. She asked if Ellen had told her what happened. Mrs. Dunn acknowledged that Ellen had indeed told her, but they had heard no news.

"The next day I went to school alone; Ellen wasn't going until they received the news of her brother Bob's death. Now back then folks around here were superstitious, and when Ellen and I saw what we thought was Bob's ghost, well, most everybody believed the worst. After school let out, I rushed home, and when I entered the house, Ellen and her mother were there.

"'Mary,' yelled Ellen, 'It's all right. Bob's coming home. He was wounded, but he's going to be okay.' Mrs. Dunn went on to explain that an Army officer had come to their home and told them Bob had been shot. He would be home in about six weeks. He had suffered a lot of pain, but was in an army hospital in Hawaii and would be fixed up. He would be discharged from the Army when he was well enough to come home. About two months later, Bob Dunn was home. He had a haunted look on his face, but he said he'd be all right in time.

"It was in late May," said Mary Morgan, "and I ran into him on the square in town. 'How are you doing Bob?' I asked.

"He smiled and said, 'I'm doing pretty good. I guess I was lucky, another inch or so and I would have had it.'

"'Bob,' I asked, 'did Ellen tell you we saw you on the bridge?'

"'Yes,' he replied. 'And I'll tell you, Mary, what happened. When I was shot and lying in a rice paddy, well, I was kind of out of it for a while. I had strange visions and thank the Lord I can't remember them all. But there was one thing I do remember. I was in a daze, and for a minute I thought I was back home. In fact, I had a vision of me standing on the bridge, just looking down at the water. Then I turned and saw you, Mary, and my sister coming toward me. Then the medics arrived, and the next thing I knew I was in a hospital. I guess I just wanted to see you before I died.'

Three years later Bob Dunn and Mary Morgan were married. The old bridge is gone now, and a new super bridge is in its place. Bob and Mary occasionally walk down by the river, hold hands, and remember their meeting on the bridge.

Willow Church

It was a warm summer evening in the rural reaches of southern Appalachia when Charles Doccery's car broke down on his way home from work. With no houses anywhere on this stretch of road and very little traffic, Charles decided if he were to get home, he'd have to walk. Cutting across Timber Ridge would lessen his trek by nearly a quarter-mile, so with a sigh, Charles pushed the car to the narrow roadside and began walking up the old logging road.

The road had been cut zigzag up the mountain and across the ridge by loggers maybe forty years earlier when the pulpwood was cut. It had become known as Timber Ridge and the Old Logger's Road. Hunters referred to them mostly because there was nothing there except woods and the foundation of the old Willow Church and the abandoned cemetery. The graves were old, and some were even sinking. As far as Charles knew, there had never been any of them tended. The descendants had probably died out themselves or moved away many years before. Several of these old, old graveyards lay sprinkled about the foothills, but this one had caused talk of ghosts and being haunted.

It was full dark when Charles came upon the backside of the old cemetery. He knew where he was because big rocks served as markers to the graves themselves. The moonlight filtered through the high branches of the trees enough for him to see the gray granite rock markers against the dark brown of the earth. Charles made his way, as best as he could, around the graves, not wanting to be disrespectful to the dead buried there. He came to the rubble of the church's foundation and, having walked a pretty good piece up the hill, sat down on some of the crumbling stone foundation to catch his breath. A breeze caught in the treetops, making a whooshing sound. Cicadas called out in the night, and off in the distance an owl hooted.

Charles drew a long breath and wiped perspiration from his brow. It was a rather spooky place there. He shivered as a prickling ran up his spine. He remembered the old tale about Willow Church. It was told to him by his grandpa that a Yankee soldier torched the church while slaves were inside. The church went up in fast flames and burned to the ground within an hour while the slaves screamed and prayed as they perished in the fire. Another church was later built on the same foundation, but it too burned to the ground in the middle of the night, and no one ever knew the reason. Charles began to feel afraid and hurriedly made his way on around the old churchyard. Hearing a noise, he turned to see a large ball of fire rise up from the cemetery and land amid the foundation's rubble. The blaze pushed skyward, and Charles could hear screams and praying—which didn't stop until he reached the safety of his own home. Charles now knew the old stories held some truth, but didn't know why he was threatened that night by something that happened way back during the Civil War.

The man, now old, said he later discovered some of his ancestors fought alongside the Yankee troops as they made their march through these southern Appalachian foothills on their way to the sea at Savannah. He wonders if the Yankee soldier that burned the church could have been one of his long-ago family members, and somehow the spirits of Willow Church knew and was perhaps seeking vengeance, or maybe giving warning that he wasn't welcome on the grounds of Willow Church.

The Moaning Mist

Lorraine Dunlap, with her brothers, Harold and David, and their parents, moved into an old house. Located on River Bend Road in Dalton, Georgia, that old house was said to be haunted. The kids were ecstatic as their new neighbors told them of eerie happenings in the large, nineteenth-century house. One of the many legends about the rambling old house was that an old witch had lived there and hidden a wooden chest full of gold coins somewhere inside the house. Many of the walls had been torn up, supposedly by treasure hunters, but no treasure was ever found.

Harold and David searched from the cellar to the attic but found nothing. They never found any sign of the witch or of the ghost until one warm autumn moonlit night. Harold, the oldest boy, slept in the middle bedroom. He had just dozed off when he was awakened by the sound of a low moan. Harold flipped on the bedside lamp. He said sometime later, "My hair stood straight up, and I was too scared to move or even breathe." Harold watched in terror as an eerie, smoky, misty image floated from the bedroom ceiling to the floor, still moaning. Then he heard the bed spring creak as if someone had sat down on the bed. Harold stared in open-eyed terror until the moaning ceased. Then he heard what he could only describe as a cackle, much like he imagined a witch's laugh would sound. By now Harold was frightened out of his wits. He jumped out of bed and tore out into the hallway screaming, waking up the entire household.

Harold's father heard the boy's weird tale and checked the youth's bedroom. He did not find anything, nor did he hear anything. "I guess the boy just had a nightmare," his father said, and everyone went back to bed. Harold, as long as the family lived in the old house, never slept in the middle bedroom again.

David, a younger teenager than Harold, boasted, "I'm not afraid of any old witch. I'll sleep in the middle bedroom." So on another moonlit night, David lay confidently in his bed, reading a book. It was close to midnight on a Friday night, and there was no school the next day, so he was still awake. David was reading when he heard a soft moan. He looked up and saw, coming down from the ceiling, a misty figure. It moaned, and when he heard the cackle, he didn't wait around but made a mad dash for the bedroom door.

"We never knew what it was that scared the boys," said sister Lorraine. "But there was one more incident, and it happened to me." Lorraine was in the kitchen ironing her daddy's shirt. The rest of the family was out in the backyard garden. It was then that she heard a noise from down the hallway. She stood the iron up on the ironing board and looked down the hallway. She didn't see anything out of the ordinary. She had just turned back to the ironing board when she heard a low moan. Then the moan turned to what sounded like a woman crying. Again she peered down the hallway and saw a misty figure fading away. She ran to her father, but he didn't find anything when he investigated.

Two weeks later, the family moved away from the horrible house. The children were glad. They had had enough of the moaning, misty figure that inhabited the house on River Bend Road.

Runaway Train

Back in the early part of the twentieth century families were large. And in each of these large families was usually a relative who was—a little different, some would say eccentric. Some folks would refer to a maiden aunt, a great-uncle, or maybe a cousin who was somewhat odd. Maybe, just maybe, these odd-seeming folk were different because they saw things with an off-center view. Another thing could have been that those around them didn't understand exactly what they were saying.

This tale, told by Harlan Boyd, fits into a strange category. Most of his aunts and uncles, who saw things in a different light, were also prophetic. It was mid-summer 1918 and World War I—the war to end all wars—was going on its bloody way. The Boyds lived in the mountains of north Georgia near the North Carolina-Tennessee border. For years, Uncle Joshua Boyd, a tall, rail-thin, white-bearded man made statements that folks mostly ignored. One hot Sunday morning at church, Josh stood and announced, "Beware! There's a runaway train bearing down on us all." Again, at the town square, Josh roared, "Beware, a runaway train is coming!" Since the train came only four times a week, folks weren't too worried. Through the summer of 1918, the old man kept up his crusade, shouting, "It's coming, the runaway train!" Later, maybe a year and a half, Preacher Kimball was heard to say, "We misunderstood what Mr. Boyd was saying. What he did say was 'It's *like* a runaway train.'"

Some say it started in Fort Leavenworth, Kansas. Others said Fort Devan, Massachusetts. Wherever it started doesn't really matter because by September 1918, eighty-five hundred people died in one major city in one week. Before it ran its course in 1919, fifty million people had died. In the United States, six hundred seventy-five thousand people succumbed, not to a runaway train, but to a runaway epidemic, Influenza.

"Yes," mused Harlan Boyd, "Great-uncle Josh saw it coming, but still, even with the warning, there wasn't much anyone could do about it. Uncle Joshua ranted and raved that folks didn't understand him. Well, I'll tell anyone folks sure listened to him after the epidemic was over. It's just that no one took him seriously before the runaway train."

In March 1919, Joshua Boyd buried his long-time wife and partner. His only comment was, "It was a ghostly whisper through the wind with the consequence of a killer tornado."

Grandma

Most children growing up in southern Appalachia have been raised within the closeness of the family unit. It was often said that children were more than enough for parents to care for—it took the entire family to get them grown. Butch Preston was such a child. Living within sight of his two aunts and uncles and his grandparents, he grew up surrounded not only by family and watching eyes, but love deep and true and everlasting. Butch viewed life as good, for a mountain boy. He had several good friends, made better-than-average grades in school, and had a little money from working in his uncle's general store on Saturdays and through the summer months when school was out.

But things changed the summer of his fifteenth year. Grandma Bets died suddenly of a stroke. The family grieved heavily, but Butch couldn't seem to give the old woman over to death. Within a year, one of his aunts and her family took the grandfather and moved to Virginia. His uncle sold the general store, as the Depression was taking hold and he was feeling the crunch early on. Butch lost an aunt, uncle, cousins, and his grandfather to a job in Virginia; his beloved grandmother to death; and his job to the Depression. Looking around at his losses, the young man grew very angry. His grades began to drop in school, and soon he began to hang out with a different crowd. His mother was beside herself with worry. It was a hot, sultry night in late summer when Butch slammed out of the house to go visit one of his new friends.

"Just hanging out at Grady's, and it don't mean we're going to do anything," he growled when his mother asked where he was going and what he was going to do.

Black clouds pressed heavy down on the mountains and thunder rumbled as Butch cranked his old car. He pulled onto the highway just as big raindrops splattered on the windshield. Lightning cracked the dark night, and Butch mashed on the accelerator. He could beat the storm, he thought. Grady's place wasn't even five miles away. Besides, he was driving east and the storm was coming from the west. The harder it rained, the faster Butch drove. In a cracking flash of blue-white lightning and a torrent of rain, the car went into a spin. A sense of dying grabbed hold of Butch, and he jerked the steering wheel. The car spun round and round on the rain-slickened road. Thunder roared, wind howled, and rain came down in driving waves. On and on the car spun and the storm raged. And in the forever of the instant, Butch waited to die.

But in a split-second, the car righted itself, the wind calmed, the thunder quieted, and the rain slackened. Butch released a long-held breath. His heart hammering in his chest, he turned to see the ghost of his Grandma Bets sitting in the passenger seat. She looked at him, her face pale and glowing. I'm dead, thought Butch, but his grandma said, "Don't worry, Butch. I'm looking after you." Lightning cracked again, and the old woman with her snowy white hair was gone. Only the stormy night remained.

The car was dead. Butch turned the ignition key over and over, but the car wouldn't crank. Finally, the battery drained, the boy climbed out into the night's storm and pushed the car to the side of the road. I'm alive, he thought, and turned back toward home. He saw things differently then. He realized his life still had some good in it. Grandma Bets had loved him and watched after him when she was alive; he figured somehow she watched after him still. As he hunkered his shoulders and walked against the storm, Butch realized that maybe death could take the body but sometimes love held the spirit.

Biscuits

Marjorie Stephenson is a good cook. Actually, she is a great cook. All through the years, her family has raved about her Sunday and holiday feasts. But there was one item that Marjorie could not, no matter how hard she tried, perfect. It was a simple little thing, but even after fifty years of marriage, she still could not make a biscuit. William Stephenson, Marjorie's husband, from day one of their marriage, had to face the fact that he would never again get his favorite food, buttermilk biscuits. All was not lost, however, and William pounced on an opportunity. He invited his mother-in-law to live with them. Now, as good a cook as Marjorie was—and she was good—her mother made one thing Majorie could not: Biscuits! Buttermilk, southern Appalachian, cathead biscuits!

Over the years, William stuffed himself with his mother-in-law's biscuits, while gorging on his wife's delicious repasts. Much as her mother tried to teach her, Marjorie just could not get the hang of biscuit-making right. And her husband, come what may, wanted his buttermilk biscuits each and every morning. Then one day the mother-in-law went into the hospital and did not return. No one mourned his mother-in-law's passing more than poor William. He would face the rest of his life without his favorite buttermilk biscuits for breakfast.

Biscuits

The day after her mother's funeral, Marjorie arose from a sleepless night at 5:30 A.M. and decided she would give making buttermilk biscuits one more shot. She puttered around the kitchen, stalling for time, and finally she said aloud, "I just can't make biscuits. That's all there is to it." Then Marjorie heard a voice from somewhere beyond the kitchen. It sounded like her mother: "Marjorie, put two cups of flour in a bowl. Oh, preheat the oven to 500 degrees. Now add a pinch of salt and . . ." Marjorie followed the instructions to the letter even though the recipe didn't sound like her mother's previous attempts to teach her how to make biscuits. Knowing she sounded foolish, Marjorie said, "Mama, this isn't the way you told me to make biscuits."

"Of course, child," Marjorie thought she heard her mother say, "I had to have something of my own." Marjorie grumbled as she realized there was no set way to make biscuits. So she used her own measurements, but her mother's ingredients. When William came down to breakfast, he had a dour look on his face.

"I don't have time for breakfast today, Honey. I'm late. I'll grab a bite at the fast food place," he said when he saw flour dustings on everything in the kitchen.

"William Stephenson," snarled Marjorie, "you will sit down there and eat the breakfast I prepared." William sat down, and Marjorie brought out eggs, just the way he liked them, hash brown potatoes, a bowl of grits, and the greatest cooking invention of all time, a platter of buttermilk biscuits.

"Sweetheart, that was the best breakfast I ever had. And the biscuits were even better than your mother's."

When her husband left for work, Marjorie looked around sheepishly and said, "Thank you, Mother." And she swears she heard, "That's all right, Marjorie. Now I will be on my way."

Marjorie is a good cook. She is also a champion buttermilk biscuit maker, at least according to her husband, William, who says she got the recipe from her mother.

The Sliding Door

Kay and Michael Deeter moved into a small tract home, one of four, in the Appalachian foothills of north Georgia. The move was a stopgap measure, just temporary, while their own new home was under construction. Kay's parents lived with them in the rental home to help as they prepared for the bigger move into their new home in the mountains. Things started to happen the very first weekend.

"We were sitting in the kitchen," said Kay, "having a late Saturday morning breakfast when we heard a crash. Dad and my husband, Michael, ran to the living room where the noise seemed to be coming from. What they found was the sliding door to the deck wide open." There was no reason for the sliding door, which had been closed, to now be open. Everyone started going through the house to see if anyone had come in.

"Hey," shouted Michael, "everybody come here in the bedroom." What the family found was what looked like blood splashed all over one wall in the bedroom.

"There was no earthly reason for blood to be on the bedroom wall," said Kay. Anyway, they washed the wall and removed whatever the red stuff was. The next Saturday the same thing happened; only this time Michael, Kay, and her Dad saw the sliding door whip open as if a tornado-like wind had hit it. They immediately called the landlord, who came right over. He couldn't explain the door flying open and was shocked when he saw the bloodstained wall.

"I'll tell you what," the shaky landlord said. "I'll have a new sliding door put on, and I'll get the wall painted. I've been having trouble in the other three houses, but it ain't nothing like this."

On Monday morning, bright and early, workmen came and replaced the sliding door. One of the workmen said, "Seems a shame to replace this door. There's nothing wrong with it." On Wednesday afternoon, the landlord's son painted the bedroom wall. And that Saturday Kay and her family, along with the landlord, sat in the living room and just waited and watched. They didn't have to wait long. Just as Kay was pouring coffee, the sliding door literally crashed open. Once again, Michael Deeter rushed to the bedroom to find the wall covered in red blood.

Ashen-faced, the landlord said, "I don't know what's going on. I think this entire tract of property must be cursed. I don't blame you folks if you want to move." Kay and Michael did move out. They rented a camper and stayed at a local resort until their new house was ready to move into. Kay's parents went back to their own home and planned to return to help the children move into the new home when the time came.

That was several years ago, and the four houses are all gone now. One burned to the ground, and the landlord bull-dozed the other three down. One local resident said, "Of course that property is cursed. The landlord was right. It was Chief Whitepath's land, and when he was forced on the Trail of Tears with the rest of his Cherokee Tribe, he cursed the land and anyone living on it."

Owl's Cry

Many old sayings, superstitions, and myths were born here in these mountains. Perhaps some were valid; maybe others offered excuses for whatever happened. Some of these old beliefs are still sworn by today. The superstitions are handed down from one generation to the next as surely as the names on family trees. Marla Smith tells of a strange tale she herself experienced some sixty years ago there in the mountains with deep hollows and high ridges growing deeper and higher the farther you go north. Marla's voice is soft as she speaks; one wonders if she will go on with the story or maybe decide to keep it secret yet a while longer.

"When I was a teenager and still living at home," Marla begins, "my sister, Judith, and her children were staying with us. Her husband, Ernest, had died, and she needed help with her kids. She'd been there for several months, and every few weeks she'd get to worrying about her house and her furniture and personal belongings. She did have some beautiful things. So she decided she'd go home and check on everything then return to stay with us for a while longer, until she could come more fully to terms with Ernest's death. He'd been killed in a car wreck. The bus ran from town to Dawsonville every day, so Judith always took the bus when she felt the need to go home for an overnight visit.

She'd leave the babies with us. Poor Judith, she was in no shape to care for them, especially since one was still on the bottle and the other two not much bigger.

"When Judith got to her home, everything was just fine, just the way she'd left it. I often wondered if maybe she just got lonesome for her house or maybe she wanted to mourn and grieve for Ernest alone, without family crowding her. Judith was there only a little while when she got real sick and had to go to bed. The next morning a neighbor stopped by to visit a bit and check to see if she and the kids were holding up okay. He couldn't get an answer when he knocked on the door and, knowing she was there because the door was slightly ajar, went inside to find Judith near death. He managed to get her into his old truck and, knowing the family, brought her back to our house as quickly as he could. The pain seemed to be mostly in her chest. I remember Mama being so worried. Dr. Johnson was sent for. He said it was pneumonia and set an oxygen tent over her. There wasn't a hospital in the community then, and any doctoring was done in the home.

"John was my sweetheart at the time, and he had come by for a short visit. He didn't know the troubles befalling us. When the doctor left, Mama sent me and John to get Mrs. Curtis, her long-time friend and neighbor, to come and help out with Judith. We didn't waste any time and left immediately for the Curtis home. It was only about a quarter-mile away. Even though it was dark that night, the moon was shining to give enough light to see by. As we stepped from the yard to the road, an owl hooted, and then as we hurriedly walked up the road toward the Curtis home, the owl kept flying in front of us to land in nearby trees and hoot its mournful cry as we passed. The owl did this all our way to the Curtis house. When we arrived, I told Mrs. Curtis of our dilemma, and she quickly informed her family of her leaving and gave instructions. She too had a house full of children, but none so young they couldn't be left. She quickly stuffed her snuff tin into her apron pocket and grabbed a wrap from a peg behind the door because the night was slightly chilled, and we hurriedly made our way back.

"The owl was waiting as we left the Curtis house and again hooted and flew in front of us and called its mournful cry as we passed. It made the same trip we did, all the way hooting and hooting as if to warn of the troubles soon to come. Once we were home, the owl perched in a tree just beyond the back porch. It gave its mournful call often during the night, and the next day Judith died. I never saw the owl or heard it at our house again.

"Later, John and I were married and we often wondered and talked about that night and the owl and thought it might have somehow been there as a warning. I still get a chill when I hear the mournful cry of a hoot owl in the night."

Minerva's House

Bob Burdick was a vagabond in his younger days. He circled the globe while a member of the United States Air Force, and when his hitch was over, he became a building contractor constructing power plants throughout the Southeast. Then at the ripe old age of forty-three, he built a sailboat and cruised the Caribbean for five years.

"Guess I always had a touch of wonder and wander about me," he says with a twinkle in his eyes and a boyish grin on his face. But Bob isn't so much the wanderer now. Open-heart surgery has slowed him down a bit, though he is far from still in his home in the foothill mountains of north Georgia.

Bob was only eight years old when he decided there was something different about his granny's house, strange and a bit eerie. But Granny was there, so he really wasn't afraid. He was making his first overnight trip to Granny's when he began to learn and experience firsthand the mysteries of Granny's house.

"It was 1944, and Dad was in the Navy," he says. "Mom had taken a second job, working nights on weekends. 'Had to make ends meet,' was the way she put it. So there I was with a pillowcase stuffed with my clothes, my Roy Rogers cap pistol with the ivory grips, and my toothbrush rattling around in Mama's tin button box. Mama said she didn't want germs on it. I wasn't thinking or caring about germs when she snapped the lid on the little box. All I could think about was the night ahead, and if I couldn't just stay at home by myself, then the only other place I'd rather be was with my granny. Cause she was sweet and fun. She knew I was a whippersnapper, she said, and loved me anyway. Her house was old and big, and I was sure there were hidden treasures there somewhere, had to be, I just had to find them."

Bob pauses in his story and stares into the distance of yesterday and childhood and smiles wistfully in remembrance. It is plain to see in his expression the woman and maybe the house that helped influence and make him the gentle person he is today. In just a flicker of time, Bob goes on with his story in soft words that are sometimes barely audible.

"It wasn't really Granny's house, but it was her home. And her living there, I found out, was the result of Minerva Bruster's dying ten years earlier. That was two years before I was even born, so I figured maybe I wasn't really and truly connected to the house by rights of law, but I couldn't help but be a little sad to discover this wasn't really my granny's own home, but a loaner. I didn't know Minerva. I heard hand-me-down tales, but the ones Granny told and things I witnessed as a boy and incidents that occurred years after when my granny passed away still give me a little sting somewhere deep inside. Seems Minerva had died in bed in this same house where she'd been born about eighty-eight years earlier. She had married her beau, Silas Bruster, in the big parlor room we now called the living room. Minerva birthed their two children, both girls, Rebecca and Prudence, in the same room, the same bed she died in. The old woman was of good health and stamina and went on to outlive her husband and both children.

"As Minerva lay on her deathbed, the room was full of

people. The doctor was present, along with his assistant, assuring those about that all hope was lost, saying they were there on a mission to make the old woman's passing as painless and easy as possible. Several young adult grandchildren waited like vultures. They'd never cared about Minerva while she lived, but now that she was dying, she held their full attention. Each was there to stake claim to their share of the Minerva Bruster estate. Minerva's lawyer was there, too, because Minerva had other plans for what was hers and this lot before her would not be rewarded. Time ran out for the old woman before a proper will could be drawn up by the attending lawyer, but everyone there heard clearly her final wishes because she made sure to speak plain and clear so there would be no misunderstandings. All Minerva's money was to go to a woman who had befriended and looked after her in the last years of her life. The home, all the furnishings, and full use of the land were also to go to this person and be used as she saw fit for as long as she lived. This person was my granny.

"In the remembering, I always thought it was strange there was never any mention of a preacher being there at Minerva's dying, but I guessed maybe she didn't want one or maybe her preacher of choice was busy with other business or something churchy. A few days after Minerva's death and funeral, the grandchildren got together and started a legal battle to reclaim the estate. But because there were other witnesses, Minerva's last wishes stood fast.

"I didn't really know much about the house and the way Granny came to be there before that first overnight visit. In the past, during short visits with Mama, my romping range had been restricted to the downstairs. But then for weekend visiting, I had full run of the house, with only one restriction: the large upstairs bedroom at the very end of the hall, the room where Minerva had died. The door to this room was always kept open, but I was not to go into this room, nor was I ever, ever to close the door. That was the rule. I thought it was kind of strange, but the words came from Granny and I never sassed or back-talked her. No, sir. What she said was the law. Besides, the house was huge with lots of narrow hallways, big rooms, and funny-shaped closets in the strangest places. This house was a kid's dream, just made for exploring and hiding. I knew I would have a world of fun even without that one old bedroom."

Bob pauses again in his storytelling and runs fingers through his short salt and pepper hair. The memories are flooding his mind. One can almost see his excitement as his eyes twinkle and that smile curls unexpectedly in the short silence. After a brief rest and something cool to drink, Bob again continues the story as if he were once again eight years old at Granny's house for his first overnight visit.

"After supper that night, Granny asked me if I'd like to walk into town for an ice cream cone. It was still daylight because Granny always ate early, and it wasn't far. And because I'd eaten all my supper and then helped wash the dishes, Granny said she'd buy me a double scoop. Two scoops of ice cream. That would cost a dime. I wondered if breakfast would bring about the same results. I quickly agreed to her offer. She didn't have to ask twice, and I sure didn't want her to change her mind.

"On the way to Whalen's Drug Store, which had the only soda fountain in town, Granny told me what all we'd be planting in the garden in a few weeks. 'Can I help?' I asked as I jumped and skipped, trying not to land on the spider-web cracks all over the town sidewalk. Granny paused a bit to pinch a tad of snuff from the little tin she kept in her apron pocket and put it between her lip and gum. When she got it wet, she nodded slowly and said, 'I reckon you're about big enough to do just that. And Lord's sake, with the both of us working, we'll have that garden planted in no time.' I was so happy I stumbled and stepped on a crack in the sidewalk. It was an accident. Seeing what I'd done, I quickly asked Granny if her back was okay. She said it was. I figured maybe there wasn't nothing to that silly song the girl next door to us sang when she jumped rope down in the road in front of our house.

"On the walk back home, we didn't talk much 'cause we were too busy licking ice cream. It was wonderful. Part of me wanted to gobble it up real fast, and the other part wanted to make it last as long as I could. I decided right then being with Granny was turning out to be lots more fun than if Mama had let me stay home by myself. The sun had gone down behind the far-off mountains when we got back to Granny's house, but a soft glow hovered over the closer hills. It was that real pretty time of day when the air gets cool, the day noise shushes, the early stars start twinkling, and lightning bugs begin to blink and flash in the tall grass. We watched all this for a few minutes while sitting on the front steps that led to a wide porch wrapping around three sides of the house. The night was so pretty and calm that it made me feel kind of lazy, but the moment we stepped inside the house, I got the willies.

"When we'd left, a big, overstuffed chair sat flat back against the wall; now it was turned around and the curtain was pulled back, just like somebody had been sitting there looking out the window. I pointed to the chair and whispered to Granny, 'A burglar's been in the house.' She looked in the direction I had pointed, shook her head, and then smiled. I figured if it wasn't a burglar, it had to be a ghost and was just about to tell Granny when she took my hand and led me to the kitchen. At the table, we had a cookie and some milk, and she told me the first story about Minerva. I could feel little feet running all over my back and up my neck as Granny spoke. When she finished, my toes were knotted up together tighter than a green-apple stomachache.

"'But Granny, how can that be? You said she's dead. Right?' I asked real soft-like.

"'Yes,' Granny answered, 'but she just hasn't moved along yet.'

"I leaned closer to Granny and whispered, 'Do you ever see her?'

"'Every once in a while, but not like we see each other,' she answered through a smile to ease my fear.

"I looked under the bed that night, and when I jumped into it, I pulled the covers up over my head. I kind of woke up sometime during the night when Granny came in to check on me and fix the covers I'd kicked off the foot of the bed. The next morning I thanked Granny for looking in on me. I also told her how thin and pretty she looked in the moonlight peeking in through the lace curtains. She looked at me kind of strange, and those little feet ran over my back and up my neck again. Granny said she hadn't come into my room the night before; then she showed me an old picture of Minerva when she was young. She was thin and very pretty.

"In the weekends that followed when I spent the night with Granny, the chair always sat flat against the wall until we left; then when we returned, we'd find it turned toward the window and the curtain pulled back. I thought maybe Granny had a way of doing this little trick. Besides, believing this was kind of funny and didn't scare me. All those thoughts changed the day Granny and I played my favorite game: hide and seek. This day I broke the rule and went into the bedroom at the end of the upstairs hall. Really, I broke two rules, because I also closed the door. When I saw where I was, I quickly left the room. But I was caught anyway. As soon as I stepped through the doorway, the door slammed shut. It wouldn't open no matter what I did. I was still trying when Granny found me. I was crying. I told her I was sorry. I was still trying to get the door open as Granny patted my back and said we'd need to get some help.

"Later that day two men came to the house with a long, two-story ladder. They climbed up and went inside the bedroom window and finally, after some moaning and groaning, the door opened. What had kept the door from opening was a giant oak dresser as big as both the men put together. Granny asked the still-sweating men to come down to the kitchen for a glass of iced tea, but before we got halfway down the stairs, the door slammed shut again. We forgot to put the doorstop back in place. After drinking their tea, the men did it all again: climbed the ladder, crawled in the window, and moved the dresser. This time when the door was opened, the doorstop was put firmly in place. The men didn't want any more tea, but kept looking back over their shoulders as they left. After the men had been gone awhile and the excitement had died down, I asked Granny about the door. That's when she told me a little more about the house.

"Seems this magnificent, old, two-story house had been designed and built by Minerva's father. And more than a few folks in the community at the time believed the man to be a might tetched in the head because the house sat at an odd angle. It was not aligned with any of the buildings around it. But this was for a special reason, Granny said. Every year on the morning of the vernal equinox, the first sunlight to clear the hills would enter a window on the east end of the long upstairs hall, strike a mirror in the bedroom at the far end of the hall, and then reflect onto another wall that had a life-sized portrait of Minerva's mother. It must have been like magic because I didn't understand it all, but I guessed if I had gone to all that trouble to get all the reflections, I wouldn't want the bedroom door closed either.

"Years went by, and the doorstop stayed put, and the door didn't close, and the dresser never moved. I was never in the house during a vernal equinox and missed the mirror trick, but Granny witnessed it a dozen times or more, missing only those years when clouds covered the sun on that special morning. The big, overstuffed chair, flat against the living room wall by the front window and the curtain did continue to move every time the house was left empty. When Granny's health began to slide, Minerva's grandchildren, many now with children of their own, were again eagerly waiting like vultures and rubbing their palms together. Land values had plummeted on that not-so-nice side of town, but the Historical Society had taken a deep interest in the old house and had money to spend. The house was said to be the last of its kind and worth more now than ever before. And the day Granny died, it would be theirs.

"That day occurred August 1, 1968. Granny's body was still at the funeral home when one of Minerva's new heirs gave notice that all of Granny's possessions had to be out of the house within the next forty-eight hours. I didn't believe these orders would stand for even five minutes if posed before a judge, but I said I'd see it was done. It was also what Granny had asked."

Bob sighs with the telling, as though he is tired and the pain of Granny's death new again. After a few deep breaths, he finishes the story.

"I spent a day packing Granny's stuff and the next moving it all out. I also had the power turned off and paid the bill up. But when I went back inside the house after the last load was out, I took one final look around and noticed the chair by the window had not moved. It was flat back against the wall and the window curtain hung straight. On the morning after Granny's funeral, I gave the house keys to the eager heirs. That same night, during an awful storm, as lightning cracked jagged, spider-web patterns across the sky, thunder roared like a thousand trains, and winds moaned in a howl of madness, the house burned to the ground. I saw it as Minerva's last act before she moved on."

Blood-Red Stain

Richard Gentry was employed by his father-in-law as a construction worker. In 1975, the crew was contacted about expanding and renovating the old Plemmons Funeral Parlor. The pay was going to be good, so the job was accepted. The old funeral home had been built in 1910, then over the years, rooms had been added on in every direction. Their job was to add on to the building, giving it a more modern, rectangular shape. They were then to knock out some of the preexisting walls to make rooms bigger and more accommodating. The three rooms upstairs in the attic, which were used for storage, were to be made into one large showroom/storage room with proper lighting for the best display of the caskets. The entire job would take at least four months as new wiring and plumbing were also the order. But first, the rooms had to be cleaned out, beginning with the attic.

The largest room held maybe two dozen modern caskets in various sizes and colors, but the room was so poorly lit that it was hard to tell if there was anything else there. For the other two rooms, Richard went prepared with flashlight and one-hundred-watt replacement bulbs for the pull-chain lights. When the lighting was corrected, it was discovered these rooms contained stacks and stacks of beautiful old, wide pine-board and box-styled coffins.

Mr. Plemmons said he wanted them gone. He had no use for them and didn't care what they did with them. The whole mess in those rooms had been his father's or grand-father's doings long years before, and the space was being wasted. Richard readily agreed to take them away. First he dismantled every box, then stacked the wood on his truck and hauled it to his barn for storage. It took five trips to complete the job. In about six months, the Plemmons Funeral Parlor had a new modern look and a new name: Rest Haven Funeral Home.

About a month later, Richard's mother, Mona, was visit-ing and saw the beautiful wood stored in the barn. "I've been wanting a family room for a long time," she said. "Would you build me one, using the wood? That is, if you don't have any plans for it already." It was the perfect use for the golden, honey-colored pine. Richard, his brother, and his stepdad decided they could do the job themselves, but Richard knew he'd be doing most of the work himself, as the others weren't construction-oriented. It took nine weekends, but finally it was finished. The wide pine boards graced a high arched ceiling, walls, and even the floor. No one would ever guess they came from coffins maybe a century old.

A few weeks later, Mona called her son and said, "Come over here. Looks like the ceiling's bleeding."

"What?" Richard exclaimed. "No way. Boards that old and dry don't bleed. Must be something else. Pine rosin would be long gone by now."

"No," Mona tried to explain. "The ceiling looks like it is bleeding. You know, blood, bright red blood."

"I'll be right there," Richard said, slamming down the phone.

It did look like new blood, as a bright red stain glared from the ceiling. Richard checked for knots, then the rest of the room to see if there were anymore such stains. There was nothing. Only the one spot about three feet around in that one place.

Blood-Red Stain

"I don't know what it is, but I'll take care of it," he said to his mother as she stood beside him staring up. Richard sanded the spot, removing all the red, then revarnished it to match the surrounding area. His mother was happy, and he was satisfied the problem was solved.

A few days later, Richard received another call from his mother. "Richard," she said in a shaky voice, "the ceiling's bleeding again. Just like before. Come over here. It's kind of scary." Richard hurried over, and together he and his mother stood staring up at what appeared to be the same red bloodstain on the high arched ceiling.

"Okay, Mother," he said. "I guess I just didn't do something right. I'll redo it." Again Richard refinished the spot, knowing full well he'd done it right the first time. He, too, was beginning to get an eerie feeling about the red stain appearing on the wide, pine-board coffin wood. With the job finished, Richard went home. The next morning his mother called again.

"It's back," she said.

"We'll just paint the ceiling," he said. "Will that be okay?"

"I guess," came the reply. "What choice do we have?"

Richard painted over the beautiful wood. The stain was gone again, and Mona was happy. But two weeks later, the stain began to bleed again and Richard was called about the problem. This time, three men from the construction crew came with Richard. They stretched lath across the ceiling, secured it, plastered it over twice, then painted again.

Two days passed, then a week, then two, and Richard's mother hadn't mentioned the stain when she called. Then one Sunday afternoon, about a month later, Richard and his wife went for an afternoon visit. Upon entering the family room, he looked up to see the same blood-red stain glaring back at him. He was shocked. There was no way this could happen. But it had. It had bled through the lath, varnish, paint, and two layers of plaster. What was it? Richard's mother walked into the room, and she too looked up. "I've decided it can stay," she said. "It's interesting to wonder what caused it. Guess there'll be lots of talk about it, but nobody will ever know for sure."

The man still wonders today what the stain was, and why it bled from the beautiful ceiling made from the wide, pine-board box coffins.

Wind Chimes

Chester Farber ran the local feed and seed store, and his wife, Polly, took in sewing in the early years here in a small mountain community town. Then the Depression came along; the feed and seed business slowed to a crawl and the sewing ceased altogether. Hard times spared no one. But during this time, to both their delight, Polly and Chester became parents of a daughter they named Nina. She was the center of her parents' lives.

When Nina was about three years old and in the toddler stage of her childhood, she took a bad fall off the high back porch of the old mountain home. Her screams pierced the mountain stillness of the summer afternoon. It was evident to Polly as soon as she reached the child that her leg was broken; the jagged bone had punctured through the muscle and skin of her right leg about halfway between her chubby little knee and foot. Polly didn't think, just grabbed the child up and began to run the half-mile to Dr. Montgomery's house, which also served as his office. Poor little Nina was unconscious when her mother ran screaming onto the porch of the doctor's home.

The break was bad, but the doctor and his assistant, his daughter, set the leg as best they could and plaster bound it to keep it secure. The doctor's young son went to

169

fetch Chester from the feed and seed store. Polly was not in good enough shape to go. She paced, prayed and cried, then berated herself for not watching her baby more closely. Dr. Montgomery told the parents the baby would be okay in time, but she had to wear the plaster cast for maybe six to eight weeks. He gave them powders to mix in water for the pain, as it was sure to hurt. He also said to keep the leg up as much as possible to prevent swelling. And not to let the cast get wet. It seemed to the parents the orders just went on and on, but finally, the doctor told Chester and Polly they could take little Nina home.

That night Nina slept little; with Polly just spent with worry and guilt, Chester held the child, rocking to and fro in the old rocking chair and singing to his pretty little Nina. "Nina's Daddy's little girl, with the pretty little curls. She can dance and sing. She can do anything." In about a week, the child had mastered the cast and it barely slowed her down. After eight weeks, it was removed. The leg was smaller than the other one and weak, but soon the accident was only a bad memory. Only Chester's little song remained, and whenever Nina was sick or hurt, she wanted her father to sing the Feel-Good song with its pretty little melody. She said it was magic and made her all better. From skinned knees and elbows to measles and on to little boys being bullies, the song fixed it all. When Nina was thirteen, her father died of a heart attack. She hurt so bad, she wanted to die too, and her father wasn't there to sing the pain away and never would be again.

Time passed, and when Nina was seventeen, she married Sam Bedford, a deputy in the Sheriff's department. They'd only been married seven months when Sam was killed by a moonshiner's bullet in a raid on an illegal still. Nina was devastated over her loss and soon bedridden; her strength, as well as her will to live, seemed to have drained right out of her. Nina lay in bed one hot, August night, almost a week after her husband's death, the humidity and heat like a dead weight and the heartache and grieving only adding to her misery. It was 2 A.M.; Nina hadn't slept at all, and the stillness and loneliness of the night were about to drive her insane. She was even considering suicide. After all, she would never be complete without Sam.

As she lay in the dark and planned how she would die, a tinkling melody broke her thoughts. It was the music of the feel-good song her father had sung to her to make better whatever it was that hurt. The sound came from outside her bedroom window. She hurried from her bed to find the music. It sounded like the wind chimes, but they were still. No breeze stirred, but the melody tinkled on and on. Nina knew it was her father and her beloved Sam come back to let her know they were fine and she too would begin to feel better. And Nina did feel better. Her health returned, and her depression left. She lived forty-three more years, but never remarried. Nina said for all her years, after that night, whenever she was sick or trouble threatened, the wind chimes played the feel-good melody to make her know all would be well. The wind chimes never moved or aged through all those years, and the melody never changed.

Graveyard Ghosts

James Buchanan is a long-time descendant of Pickens County, Georgia, where the Appalachian foothills begin their long range north. It is beautiful country, but it also has an eeriness that maybe was born here with the mountains and will remain as long as they themselves do. James laughs, telling a story he heard his daddy, Hansel, tell many times over when James himself was a boy.

"The family lived past an old church and cemetery when Daddy was a boy. The old dirt road was to the very edge of the burial ground. This, I'm sure, made it easy for the pallbearers when time came to lay another body to rest. They didn't have to carry the casket so very far, and there were some in the community that were of enormous size. I think Daddy must have been scared a few times getting home because Granny was always telling him if he ever really saw a haunt or ghost, or anything of that nature, he should just walk straight up to it and raise a hand and touch it, then it would disappear, never to bother him again.

"Well, this one time, Daddy was coming home just past dark. It had rained, a summer rain, so it was hot and the mist was swirling and drifting all about the gravestones. He was spooked having to go past all those dead people, but it was the only way to get to the house. Daddy began to walk, watching everywhere around him. His heart began to beat hard against his ribs when he saw something big and white rising up about middle ways into those gravestones of various shapes and sizes. It was a true ghost, and it was coming straight toward him. Remembering his mama's words, Daddy knew if he didn't banish it, it would surely get him. So in the fear and trembling of youth, he took a few deep breaths and began walking toward the ghost in the graveyard. About six feet from the apparition, he raised his hand to touch it, just as his mother had said to do. But as he reached, it made a deep whooshing sound and disappeared. Daddy said he didn't remember getting out of the cemetery, but get out he did. When he got home, he was running so fast he couldn't stop or even slow down and busted the door latch off the door getting into the house. He didn't tell the family about his scare, just went on to bed, but he didn't sleep any for thinking about the ghost.

"In the next day's morning light, things looked different. Daddy decided he'd just go to the cemetery and have a look around and see if there was anything there. Sure enough, there on the far end of the old cemetery, a big, old, white cow stood grazing on the new summer grass. It whooshed a deep breath when Daddy got close to it. He recognized the sound as being the same one he'd heard the night before. What he couldn't explain was how it disappeared before his very eyes when he reached a hand to touch it, there in the dark and mist that drifted and swirled about the gravestones."

The Haunted Tree

Seems every ridge and hollow in the southern Appalachian foothills has its own name. Some names fit, like Stover Mountain, because the Stover family has lived there as long as anyone can remember or records have been kept. Some places have lost the reason for their name; the stories birthing the names have died through the passing of time, yet the names have remained. An example is in Fannin County, Georgia. In the far reaches of Georgia, near the Tennessee–North Carolina border, a small church, Mount Agony, is located between Hell's Hollow and The Devil's Den.

Evelyn Prince Dockery has lived her entire life there, embraced by the foothill mountains of southern Appalachia with its strange names for places and landmarks. She tells stories that she remembers and experienced in the early 1900s in the foothill mountains she calls home.

This story took place in 1942, near the old haunted tree in McGee Town, Tennessee. Evelyn and her cousin, Lucy, were going up the road to Lucy's house. They had to pass right by the haunted tree, and it was late in the day. It was a scary place, especially if you were young and the sun had fallen behind the mountains. When the girls got close to the haunted tree, they saw a man sitting against it. A chill crept over them. When they were about to pass the tree, the man stood up. He

174

had no head. He wore a black suit, white shirt, and dark tie. He had a shotgun and walked about with the gunstock on top of his booted foot. Lucy and Evelyn stopped—dead still. The chill had turned to terror, ice-cold and paralyzing. The man began walking toward them, headless, the shotgun held braced on top of his foot by a heavy ham-sized hand. When he reached the girls, Evelyn screamed, breaking their paralyzed state. Lucy ran one way, and Evelyn another. The girls were scared almost to death.

When Evelyn told her parents what she had seen and where, her father wanted the mother to whip the girl for telling untrue tales. But Evelyn's grandmother and an aunt were visiting at the time and they said, "You'd better not whip that child. She's telling the truth. We've both seen it too."

The Floating Casket

Eddie Dockery remembers when he and his wife lived at Buck Fry Hollow. They didn't have a car; anyway, the road leading to their small house was little more than a wagon trail with big rocks, rain-washed gullies, and tree roots growing on top of the ground.

About two in the morning, Eddie was walking home from his job. He was tired, but with sleep and food, he would be ready for another day come morning. Just as Eddie made the last turn in the bend of the trail, from out of nowhere a casket floated out in front of him. Eddie knew he was tired, but not addled in his mind—or influenced by moonshine. It was really happening. He tried to see what was inside the floating casket, which he saw was open. But before he could get close enough to see inside, it floated higher, just beyond his reach. The casket continued to float in front of Eddie almost all the way home, then it just disappeared. The man was scared near beyond words as he tried to tell his wife of his experience. But Eddie Dockery never saw the floating casket again.

Residents

In the winter of 1946, Evelyn and Eddie were looking for a place to live in Mineral Springs, Tennessee. Eddie found a house on the outskirts of town. It was small, but the couple didn't really need a lot of room. It was old, but in fair shape. The roof was sound and the floor sturdy. The yard would be nice in the spring, and the big old Oak tree would afford a nice shade and cool breeze in the heat of summer. In the back, a vegetable garden would be just right. If nature cooperated, Evelyn could put up vegetables for the winter months. From the looks of the fruit trees and grape vines, they should have fruit—applesauce, peaches, or jelly—on the table every meal.

Eddie and Evelyn went to look at the house one Sunday afternoon. Evelyn was quite smitten with the place, so the next day, Eddie went to the owner and asked if he would rent it. The man was somewhat hesitant, even negative, but Eddie persisted, saying they would fix up anything that needed fixing and share the summer's garden harvest. The man finally shook his head and said, "You won't stay because the door won't stay closed."

Eddie laughed and said, "We'll manage to keep it closed if you'll just rent it to us."

The man reluctantly agreed. By week's end Eddie and

Evelyn were moved in. The first night they stayed there, the door somehow opened about a foot. Eddie put a lock on the door, but every time they left and came back, the door would be open, almost as if laughing at the young couple. Somewhat befuddled, Evelyn and Eddie decided to push the bed up against the pesky door. That would keep it shut. Every morning they would wake up cold because the door would have somehow moved the bed while they slept and be open, letting the cold winter air inside. Eddie then hammered big nails into the wall and bent them over the door, but the door was always open when morning came. The tale was that a man had hanged himself in the doorway of the house and maybe was still there, his body pushing against the door.

The young couple moved out of the house during the third week to a boarding house up the road a ways. This place had lots of rooms to rent, and there was a big old wraparound porch for visiting. One spring day several folks were sitting on the porch when rain began to fall. Everyone sat, dry and comfortable, and listened to the rain beginning to beat down on the tin roof. As the raindrops grew heavier, drops of blood also fell and dripped onto the front steps, the run-off making a great puddle of red blood on the ground. It was said a man had been killed there, spilling his life's blood on the steps of the boarding house.

Evelyn says in a trembling voice, "I still can't stop the shaking I get when I think about all that blood, even today."

Two Brothers

This story has been around these old mountains for years; names have been forgotten, as have time and place, yet is believed to be true by the mountain folks who know it.

There were two brothers who lived together their entire lives. One was big and strong; the other little and sickly. Neither ever married, and they had only each other for companionship. But the bigger brother, a bully, was always mean to his sibling. He would jump on the small man's back and wrestle him to the ground. This, according to the teller, was the stronger brother's favorite torture to inflict on his smaller brother. This went on for many years.

One day the weak little brother died. The bigger brother was now alone for the first time in his life. It wasn't long until the remaining brother was humpbacked and stooped low. Someone asked what had happened to cause his back to have the big hump and why did he not stand up straight anymore. The brother said the very day his sickly brother died, he felt the weight on his own back, day and night. There was never a time the weight of the dead brother wasn't there on his back even as he worked, ate, or slept. He said he was so very tired of carrying the weight around. In his anguish, he had even pulled out his eyebrows and eyelashes. But the man carried the weight of his brother on his back for the rest of his life.

Footprints

The Jackson kids just never got along. From their earliest time together, they fought. Ted, the oldest, argued daily with Theresa as long he lived. Theresa was just as argumentative as Ted. Stomping her foot, she would battle him to the end. One cold wintry night there was a party at a neighbor's house. It was about eleven o'clock when Ted became ill. Theresa held him in her arms while the guests waited with concern for the ambulance to arrive. It turned out Ted had a bad congenital heart condition. He died in the ambulance on the way to the hospital.

Four days after Ted's funeral, Theresa was in bed asleep. She awoke in the middle of the night and a strange sensation came over her. She was having an out-of-body experience. She saw herself get out of bed and go into the living room. There she saw her brother Ted sitting on the sofa. She walked over and sat down beside him. They talked for a while; then both apologized to each other for their stupid arguments over the years. They talked until just before dawn, when Ted stood and softly said goodbye. He then went out the front door.

It was snowing as Ted walked off the front porch. Theresa watched as he turned left and walked around the house. Theresa went to her bedroom and to sleep. When she arose two hours later, she looked out the window and saw footprints in the snow. Quickly she grabbed her old robe and slippers and hurried outside. The footprints circled the house but never left the area. They both started and ended there at the front porch. Theresa went to her brother Ted's room and took his shoes and went back outside. She put the shoes in the footprints there in the frozen snow. They fit perfectly.

Epilogue

With the start of the twenty-first century, the old ways are gone. Not many nineteenth-century folks are left, and many of the twentieth-century people have passed on. What this means is many of the old tales and legends are gone, too. We, the writers of this book, are trying to find as many of the old legends as we can because it is our heritage.

And we have found many stories from the southern Appalachian foothills. With computers, we have gathered many tales and saved them so we can tell people about the old ways. Nevertheless, in the foothills some things never change even if we have many new neighbors. Church is still important, as is the kitchen garden. But let's face it: while we hunt down the legends, our former serene life is changing. We are almost a suburb of a major city. Still, we'll continue to dig up tales that were once told by great-uncles, maiden aunts, and grandparents. That's our heritage.